Anglo-Nubian Goats A

Anglo-Nubian Goats Owners Guide.

By

Edward Dunbarn

Table of Contents

Introduction

The Anglo Nubian Goat is a British breed of domestic goat which was introduced when native British milking goats were bred with a mixed population of large lop-eared goats imported from India, North Africa and the Middle East.

As they adjust well to hot climates and are also good for meat production they became popular for exporting.

Anglo Nubian goats are also popular for milk production and whilst they don't produce as high a quantity as other dairy breeds their milk contains more butterfat and as a result is more flavourful.

In recent years these animals have started to attract domestic pet owners who want a pet they can interact with but which are a little bit more exotic than the usual dog or cat.

The Anglo Nubian goat was recognised as an independent goat breed in 1896 and breeders used to distinguish between them and the Nubian goats which were of African, Middle Eastern and Indian origin. Nowadays however the difference is really just semantics, especially outside of the UK, as a lot of Anglo Nubian goats were exported and bred with Nubian goats and so you will often find that they are all now referred to simply as Nubians.

Chapter 1: The Anglo Nubian Goat

The main identifying features of the Anglo Nubian Goat are the large rounded 'Roman' nose and the long, droopy, bell shaped ears.

These goats have long, deep bodies and an upright stance.

Size
These are one of the tallest and heaviest goat breeds and a fully-grown male Anglo Nubian Goat will weigh around 175lbs (79kg) and will be a minimum height of 89 centimetres (35 inches) measured at the withers.

A fully grown female will weigh approximately 135lbs (61kg) and will be a minimum height of 76 centimetres (30 inches) from the withers.

Colours And Coat
Their coat is short, fine, soft and silky.

There are a large number of variations in colour with the most common being tan, black, white and red and any solid or multi-coloured coat is acceptable by show breed standards. However as there are so many different colour combinations these animals often have lovely marbled, mottled or tortoise shell coats which make these animals even more attractive and unusual.

Life Span

If given the proper care and assuming they don't develop any serious medical issues then an Anglo Nubian Goat can live, on average, between 10 and 14 years.

Which Should I Choose?

Definitions

Kid – A baby goat up to the age of one year, can be male or female. Also referred to as Buckling (male) or Doeling (female).

Nanny or Doe – A female

Buck – A male

Wether – A neutered male

When choosing a goat you may be wondering whether you should choose a male or female or if you should go for a younger goat rather than an older one. As with anything, there are advantages and disadvantages to all.

If you are a first time goat owner it is recommended that you start with an adult or late adolescent, as they are easier to care for than babies.

With regards to sex, does or wethers are good because they tend to be more docile, friendly and content amongst their own herd. For this reason, many breeders will recommend buying either a doe or a wether if you want a family pet or a companion animal for a horse or other livestock. Wethers tend to be less aggressive than does, but are thought to be at higher risk of developing kidney or bladder stones, which could result in costly vet bills.

Of course if you are looking for a milk producer, then you will need a female.

An intact male will protect your herd from predators but many experts will caution against keeping bucks as pets as they tend to be more aggressive and harder to handle. These goats are large and heavy compared to miniature breeds such as Pygmy Goats but whilst they may not run at an adult that is taller than them, if you have children or are putting your new goat with other animals then a buck's temperament may not be suitable. Of course all animals are different, much like humans and you can't tar them all with the same brush; one buck may not act in the same way as another but it would be wise to err on the side of caution just to be safe.

The other case against bucks is that they have some disgusting and annoying habits when they are in rut. Not only do they become very aggressive, but they are also very smelly. To attract a female they will urinate on their front legs and faces, which leads to their faces and beards becoming crusty over time, making them very unpleasant to pet or handle.

Does The Anglo Nubian Goat Make A Good Pet?
Yes!

With their long ears and large noses these goats are adorable and it is very easy to fall in love with them.

Not only that but they have lovely temperaments and are friendly, sociable and outgoing. They love being around humans and can be very affectionate, some have even been known to call for their owner when they want attention.

It may come as a surprise to some people but these animals are very intelligent, in fact the Anglo Nubian Goats may be the most intelligent of all the goat breeds and you can train them to do all kinds of things. This can be lots of fun if you want to teach them tricks, especially if you have children but you can also teach them to do useful things, for instance, if you use a milking stand to milk your your goats or trim their hooves, if you show them the correct way to leave their shelter and climb onto the stand you will soon find that they can do it by themselves and will be waiting for you in the correct spot when you go out to them.

These goats are fairly hardy and can adapt to all climates and seasons as long as they are given the proper care and housing which means that as long as you understand their needs and how to meet them they can be pretty easy to keep as pets.

If you are just wanting a couple of goats as back garden pets then you probably don't have lots of other animals running about your yard but it is worth noting that goats are great company for other livestock such as horses, sheep, donkeys, cows, llamas and so on.

An added bonus to the Anglo Nubian Goats is that they are a dairy breed and their milk is delicious thanks to its high butter fat content, mentioned earlier. If you want to have your own fresh milk supply then this is a great way to get it. Many people say that milk from these goats is a lot nicer than cow's milk, not only that but those that have an intolerance to cow's milk find that they can drink goat's milk without any issue.

So there you have it, Anglo Nubian Goats do make great pets and many people say so *but* is an Anglo Nubian Goat right for you? This depends on what you are looking for in a pet. If you want one that you can keep indoors and snuggle up to whilst watching the television then these probably aren't the pet for you. Despite what some people will say these are very much an outdoor kind of pet and even though you may see lots of pictures on the internet of cute goats sat on people's sofas or cuddled up on the bed, keeping them inside is just cruel.

Whether these goats are right for you also depends on how much space you have available on your property. These goats are fairly big and they need quite a lot of space to live in. They cannot simply be tethered to a fence or cooped up in a small shed; they need a shelter that is roomy enough for them to comfortably spend time in, especially if you live in a country that gets a lot of rain. Goats are also active and will need space to run about and play in, not only to occupy themselves but also to exercise and stay healthy. As they are intelligent they get bored very easily and a bored goat is a naughty goat!

As Anglo Nubian Goats are herd animals you have to have at least two of these animals in order for them to be happy; for some this can be a drawback, for others it's simply an excuse to buy more goats!

Whilst goats can live comfortably with other animals it is not recommended to keep them with dogs. Some people do claim to keep their goat with a dog with no problems, but some dogs see them as prey. Sometimes a goat's playfulness ignites a hunting instinct in a dog causing them to chase and hunt the goat which can, more often than not, end in disaster.

If you do intend to buy an Anglo Nubian Goat then you will need to be prepared to commit to them for the long term which means you should consider what you will do with them should you wish to have a weekend break or a longer holiday. Whilst you can easily board a dog in kennels it may be far more difficult to find a carer for a goat.

One last consideration is that you will need an experienced livestock vet for these animals. If they are cared for properly you hopefully should never need medical care for them but no matter how good an owner you are there is always a chance that your goat will get sick so it would be wise to find out if there is a suitable vet nearby before you purchase your animals.

As long as an Anglo Nubian Goat suits your home and lifestyle then there is no reason why you shouldn't keep them as pets, they can pretty much do what cats and dogs do in terms of petting, playing and interacting with humans but are slightly more unusual.

One Goat Or Two?

As mentioned above, these are herd animals therefore buying one goat is not recommended. Whilst they can be great companion animals for other livestock they will thrive far better with another goat.

A lone goat is not a happy goat and you will find that they will be noisy and stressed which will eventually lead to serious health problems so you should have at least two goats.

Of course this means that you will need at least double the space, food, time and attention, as well as the extra costs you will incur so you should take this into consideration before you buy any goats.

You should also consider their lifespan – if you're lucky your goats will live a very long life but if one dies before the other you would need to replace it rather than leave the remaining goat by itself. This isn't as simple as it sounds as you will need to be cautious when introducing new goats to each other or other animals as, like people, they have their own personalities and may not always take to each other however whilst people can avoid anyone they don't like a goat may just lash out and it could lead to injury or death for one or both of your goats.

Owning goats is a big commitment which, if you love them is not a problem but if you are not sure then I would advise you think about it a little bit more before rushing into anything.

Cost

The cost of purchasing and owning an Anglo Nubian Goat is dependent on the type of goat you buy and whether you purchase everything new or whether you recycle, repurpose or get items for free.

Are you going to buy a registered goat or an unregistered goat? If you are buying pets that you are never going to breed or show then there is no reason why you can't go for ones that are unregistered, especially if they are going to spend the rest of their days with you as a pet. If you want Anglo Nubian Goats that you can breed or that are of high show quality or milking standard then you may want to pay a bit more for them. Just be aware that if you bought an unregistered goat then you may find it harder to rehome them if you found that you needed to do so at a later date for whatever reason. Also if you do decide to breed you will not be able to register the kids unless the adult goats were registered.

The next decision you have to make is whether you want a doe, a wether or a buck as this will also effect the price, for instance, an intact male that could be bred or a doe of breeding and milking age will be far more expensive than a wether.

Another cost factor is whether you buy on a pre-loved or second hand website or if you buy directly from an established breeder. On these second hand websites you can pick up goats that people wish to re-home due to circumstances in their life, for instance, if somebody has bred their goats and have decided to keep the female babies they may be selling their buck to avoid in-breeding. Whilst a lot of these sellers are genuine I would always be wary and visit the goat in person and check that they have all their vaccinations, et cetera up to date before committing to buy.

Price wise, from a breeder a registered, pure bred Anglo Nubian intact buck or doe will cost you around £450 ($587). An unregistered Anglo Nubian will cost around £250 ($326) upwards. However some people are selling these animals online for as little as £100 ($130) although I would be cautious if buying so cheap.

The next expense after your goat will be fencing. Again this could cost as low as £50 ($66) if you can get the materials for free or use repurposed items, or it can cost you upwards of £300 ($400) if you want an elaborate set up. It also depends on where you live and how much space you have for the enclosure.

Likewise is housing – I've known people who have built their goat sheds from sheets of corrugated iron and pallets that they've picked up for free, whilst others have paid out hundreds of pounds on a brand new shed. Whether you are planning to breed or not will need to be considered because if you are you may want to put in stalls so your goats can be separated when needed and it is better to do this at the beginning than further down the line. Climate will also play a part in this cost; if you live somewhere that is hot all year round you won't need as expensive a shed because your goats will be able to live outside most of the time, whereas if you live somewhere that is often rainy and cold then your goat shed will need to be warm and free from draughts and it will also need to be big enough to house some goat toys to keep your new pets occupied if they are going to be spending a lot of time in there.

Your next consideration is goat toys – again you can get kids' slides and play houses or pick up wooden pallets or spools for free or you may choose to buy these. I would always use second hand items if possible for goats, as it will eventually get dirty and broken.

A hayrack is a must have item so that your goats are not being fed directly from the floor as if they ingest faeces then it could lead to illness, In the UK you can buy a hayrack for as little as £30 upwards depending on the size and quality. In the US, a hay feeder can cost you anywhere from $40 upwards.

A full sized Anglo Nubian Goat will eat around 5lbs of hay per day which will equal out to around 50 bales or more per year. Of course this amount may vary per household depending on how wasteful your goat. They may also eat less hay if they have more forage and vice versa so someone who has large acres of land will probably use less than somebody who is keeping goats in a small back garden.

In the UK, you can feed each goat for around £20-£30 each month. In the USA, costs can be as low as $20-$30 per month. Remember these costs are PER GOAT so you will need to double this for two.

Bedding can cost you around £10/$10 depending on the area in which you live. How much you use will depend on how often you change it; if you do lots of spot checks each day and only do a full change once a month then you can keep costs low. Also if you live in a hot climate you will most likely use less bedding because firstly you won't need as much to keep your goats warm and secondly they will most likely be outdoors more therefore it will stay cleaner for longer.

The final costs to factor in are things like de-worming and vet bills. These are dependent on how much your vet charges, how often you take them and the reasons for going. A general yearly check-up for instance could cost you £50 per goat or a more serious problem could cost you a few hundred pounds. (Likewise in the USA it could cost you $20 to $250 depending on why you are going and how often). As these prices are per goat I would advise that you either look into getting your goats insured or put away a certain amount of money each month just in case you do need to take them to a vet for any reason. Many goat owners struggle with insuring because they are not sure what to class them as but often goats are insured under the umbrella of exotic pets so check with the insurer just to be sure otherwise you may find they refuse to pay out should a problem occur.

The remaining costs are things like leashes, collars, hoof trimmers and so on, which are all one-off costs and again can cost you from £50 (or $65) for the whole lot depending on whether you buy second hand or new and whether you opt for high quality or not.

All in all I believe that the costs for owning a couple of Anglo Nubian Goats are higher in the beginning when you have to purchase your fencing and housing, etc. but can be kept low each month when you are only purchasing food and a few supplements here and there.

However they are by no means the cheapest pet, especially because you need a minimum of two, and your initial costs for housing, fencing, toys and equipment, as well as the goats themselves will be fairly high so it would make sense to start saving first and then purchase your goats when you have adequate fencing and housing in place ready for them.

Chapter 2: Laws

Before you rush out and buy your adorable new pet you should consider the law in your area. Are goats even allowed on your property? If you're renting, it may have crossed your mind to ask permission from the landlord and if you own your house then you may nod and say "of course, I own my property and land therefore I can bring any animal I wish to live there", however it may not be this simple.

Anglo Nubian Goats are first and foremost farm animals and whatever country you live in they will be treated as livestock by the authorities. The phenomenon of keeping goats as pets is still relatively new and even if you class your goat as a treasured family member you should be aware that there are numerous rules and regulations you must comply with.

UK

If you are moving to or live on a newly built area then most likely you will be prohibited from owning livestock such as goats and chickens.

In the UK, if goats are allowed onto your property then you must have a holding number (CPH) for your property as well as a herd number in order to own a goat. The good news is that whilst this may sound daunting, it is simply a matter of contacting your local DEFRA (Department for Environment, Food and Rural Affairs) office and filling out a form. There isn't even a charge.

You are also required to keep a holding register for your goats, which is essentially a record book that details every movement of individual animals to and from your land. You will need to record any births or deaths in this book also. It can be a paper record, which is obtained from DEFRA or can be completed online using the ARAMS (Animal Reporting And Movement Service) website. Again, whilst time-consuming, it is pretty straightforward.

When you get to the stage of finding goats to purchase, you should check that the animals you want are properly identified with ear tags and/or a tattoo that shows the herd number as well as the goats' individual numbers, as goats cannot leave their birth premises unless they are identified. This is the responsibility of the breeder but because it is illegal to move a goat that is not properly earmarked it is important that you, as the buyer, check that this has been done before purchasing.

Once you have purchased your goats and are ready to move them to your land you should be handed a copy of the Animal Movement License (AML), which you should return to Trading Standards (Animal Health) within three days of moving the goat onto your land.

Each year you will also need to do an inventory of all livestock on your land, even if you only have a couple of goats as pets.

If you decide that you no longer want to keep goats, whether it's because they died and you don't wish to replace them or because you choose to sell them on, you will have to inform APHA (Animal and Plant Health Agency) within thirty days of the goats no longer being on your land.

Keeping medical records for goats is a legal requirement and these should include vaccinations and any medicines that are administered to each individual animal.

Another law is that of the disposal of fallen stock. Not only do you have to record the death in your holding register but you need to dispose of your goat either by taking it to a pet crematorium yourself or by arranging for a licensed collector to visit your home. If you choose the latter you must keep the receipt with your records. You are not allowed to simply bury your goats on your land.

Please check the laws in your local area regarding keeping these animals as pets before you purchase them. Whilst the information contained in this book is correct at the time of going to press, the legal requirements for keeping livestock change constantly and it is advised that you contact your local DEFRA office to ensure you have the most up-to-date information before bringing goats onto your land.

USA

In the US, you should check the zoning requirements for your town/city, as some don't allow for goats or any livestock to be kept as pets. This information can be obtained from your local zoning board office or building inspector.

Be prepared to wait a while for them to come back to you with an answer because the 'keeping goat as pets' craze is still fairly new. As the municipal ordinances were drawn up many moons ago when goats were classed as farm animals, not pets, they are usually only accepted in the zoning districts that are classed as agricultural and prohibited in those areas that are seen as residential.

Animals are usually regulated in several ways, so you should also check the general city/town ordinances or by-laws, especially any that deal with 'nuisance' animals and animal control, as sometimes goats are expressly prohibited as 'nuisance animals'.

If you are living in a city that bans the larger breeds of goats like the Anglo Nubians then you should check the rules for the miniature breeds as some will allow these. However be aware that even if your city allows goats, you also need to check your homeowners association or condominium rules if these apply to you because there may be explicit rules there.

Areas that allow goats may have specific rules regarding their care. This can include (but is not limited to) the following:

- All goats must be dehorned and male goats must be neutered.
- Only two goats are allowed (no more and no less).
- The type of shed used to house the goats should meet specific requirements with regards to size, design and so on.
- The shed must have direct access to an outdoor enclosure, which should also follow strict guidelines with regards to the

size (usually at least four hundred square feet), specified design, height of the fencing and so on.

- Droppings must be removed and properly disposed of in a manner that prevents health issues, pests (such as flies) and water contamination.
- Selling goat-derived food products such as milk or meat is prohibited.

Again the above rules will vary between towns, cities and states and there may be many more that aren't mentioned here. My advice is to check before you buy and don't break the law.

Whilst it can be frustrating to be told you can't have the pet you desire or to be waiting weeks or even months for an answer, remember that it can be just as confusing for the authorities to interpret the antiquated rules when it comes to keeping goats as pets.

If you do initially get turned down, don't be discouraged. It is possible in some circumstances to get the rules changed, for example, a girl that suffered with anxiety was allowed to keep a pygmy goat by stating it was a doctor recommended companion animal. Whilst I'm not suggesting you run to the doctors just because you have been told you can't have a couple of Anglo Nubian Goats, the example does highlight the fact that rules can be changed and as the rules were made before goats became pets it may be worth writing to your local council member, showing evidence that they are now classed as 'backyard' pets and asking if they can look at the laws and help you get permission to keep a couple of these animals.

Neighbors

You might not ordinarily care what your neighbors think about what you do but you should, out of courtesy, consider how your neighbors feel about you keeping goats in your back garden.

Anglo Nubian Goats have a reputation for being loud and whilst it is usually because they want something, the noise may still annoy your neighbours, especially if they are bleating because they want your company and you are out at work all day.

Secondly, goats smell. They are farm animals after all, and your neighbors may not appreciate the odor that emanates from your yard once your new pets arrive, especially when the weather is warm.

Thirdly, piles of manure not only looks unpleasant but an untidy enclosure can attract flies and other pests which again, can become a nuisance to your neighbors should they wish to sit out in their backyard.

Goats are also great escape artists and your neighbors may not be very happy to find that your goat has gotten out and eaten their prize roses or taken the washing off their line.

Any of the above could lead to friction between you and your neighbors and could result in them reporting you to the authorities or in some extreme cases could lead to them taking matters into their own hands.

I would suggest you have a conversation with all your neighbors before you purchase your goats and if they have any reservations reassure them that smells, noise, and so on will all be dealt with immediately before the goats become a nuisance to them. If you have a good relationship with your neighbors then they probably won't mind, as long as they know that you will clean up the mess and it won't affect them. If they don't then whilst it is entirely up to you (assuming the authorities are allowing it), I would think carefully about whether it is worth alienating your neighbors just because you want a couple of goats.

Chapter 3: Before Buying

Research

This is something I would always recommend to anyone regardless of what pet they are buying, but I believe it is especially important for creatures like these that are not traditional pets like cats and dogs.

Reading books such as this one and visiting websites is a good start but you should also join forums and social media groups that are dedicated to Anglo Nubian Goats and ask questions to find out the ins and outs of buying and caring for these animals.

If you haven't found a breeder then ask for recommendations, but even if you have found a breeder you are happy with it is worth asking whether anyone has heard of them, as someone else may have used them and can tell you both good and bad things about them.

Connecting with other goat owners before you buy is great because you are building up a network that you could then use should you buy a goat and need help or advice in the future. Often owners are happy to share their knowledge and experience and some may even offer to speak to you via the telephone to answer any questions you may have.

I would also advise that you speak to a vet that specializes in Anglo Nubian Goats and ask them for advice on what to look for when you are purchasing. They may also have a price list so that you can get an idea of the cost of both buying these creatures as well as vet bills in your area. This is a good way to ensure you are not being ripped off with your initial purchase and can also give you an indication of whether you can afford to keep these animals in the long-term or not.

Registered Or Unregistered?

It is always better to purchase a registered goat if possible because they have lineage that can be tracked, similar to a 'pedigree' dog. You will be able to see all the background records. This not only means you can enter them into pet shows but from a breeding point of view, makes the goats easier to sell. If you have it in mind to breed your goat in the future then you should always buy a registered goat, as more people are looking to purchase registered animals these days. If you breed two goats that are not registered then the kids cannot be registered so always check when you are purchasing that all the goats in the herd have been registered. In addition, should your circumstances change, which means that you have to re-home your pet, it will be a lot easier to do so if your goat has been registered as the new owners may want to breed them.

A registered goat costs more, which is a disadvantage for someone looking for a pet, however it also means that if you do breed or sell your goat it will be worth more. For instance, an unregistered Anglo Nubian Goat will be on the market for £100-£250 (around $130-$326) whereas a registered one can be sold for anything from £100-£450 or more (Approximately $130-$587) depending on age, lineage and whether they are breeding stock or show quality.

However, the flipside of course is that if you are just looking for a couple of pets then do you really need a registered goat? You may want to save the money and not bother if you have no intention to breed or show them.

Questions To Ask A Breeder

It is important that you know what to look for when purchasing an Anglo Nubian Goat so that you can be certain that you are buying a healthy animal.

Write down a list of questions that you want to ask the breeders before you decide whether to purchase or not. These should include (but are not limited to) the following:

Have the goats all been tested for CL, CAE and Johnes? If the answer to this question is no then leave immediately! Most likely the answer will be yes, in which case you should ask the breeder to provide you with the results. Never take a seller's word no matter how friendly and trustworthy they appear to be. A genuine seller will care about their animals and will be happy to provide any evidence to prove that they are healthy. Some goat breeders will test the goat that they are selling but really you should ask to see results for the whole herd.

What goat organization is the breeder registered with? There are many to choose from and there isn't really one that is better than the other but all breeders should be associated with a goat organization so that you can be reassured that their goats are registered. In the UK, the main one is The British Goat Society and in America, the big one is the ADGA (American Dairy Goat Association) although there are others so it is worth asking as you could always check directly with the society that the goats have been registered and the sellers aren't just trying to sell an unregistered goat at a higher cost. It is worth noting that the Anglo Nubian Goat Society is a not for profit organization rather than a society that registers goats and runs shows.

Can I have photographs? This only really applies if you are searching online and enquiring via email rather than viewing the goats in person but it is probably a good idea to ask for pictures before travelling a long way to view the goats anyway. Don't settle for just one picture but decide which goats you are interested in, then ask the breeder to send you photographs of these goats from different angles so that you are able to see that they are healthy and in good condition.

Can I see the paperwork? If you are buying a registered goat it is advised that you ask the breeder to have all the paperwork ready so that it can be passed over at the time of the sale. If you are not collecting your goats in person then ask them to email you a copy (or send a photograph of the paperwork via text or messaging app) so that you are certain it is all ready and waiting. There are lots of stories on the Internet of people who have been fobbed off by breeders promising to send paperwork only to discover months (or even years) down the line that the paperwork never existed and the goat has never been registered yet you have paid the higher price.

You may also want to ask about the appraisal and production records, as these will tell you how several of the goat's characteristics stack up in comparison to other's in their herd, which may be important if you do want to breed or show these animals.

What is the personality and pedigree of the goats like? As mentioned previously, a registered goat should mean you can trace their lineage and the breeder should be able to provide details of their pedigree.

It is important that you ask about the goats' personalities so that you can find one that is suited to you and your home. For instance, if you want a family pet then you should tell the breeder this and they should have an idea of which of their goats will be suited to children and which ones might not.

I would always recommend that you visit the goat yourself before buying so that you can see if you are compatible. Some goats are standoffish whilst others are downright unfriendly. If you can meet the goat first you will get an idea of whether you like it or not. In addition, goats will like certain people and not others, so you may have a goat that is described as 'standoffish' yet when you meet it may take a liking to you and you may discover that it is more affectionate than you thought, likewise, the same is also true; one that has affectionate parents may take an instant disliking to humans and not want to bond with you.

Once you meet a goat you can decide whether or not you have time to work with them or whether they are too temperamental and you won't be able to train them. If you've never had goats before, once you've visited a breeder you may decide that they are too noisy or too smelly and are not suitable for the area in which you live. It is better to discover this before you purchase than afterwards.

What food have the goats been eating? It is important to know what food the goats have been raised on. Some breeders will give you an extensive list and specific brands and may even provide you with a couple of weeks' worth of food, but if they don't you should make sure you are clear about what the goats have been eating and if possible, where you can purchase either the same food or similar. This is because a dramatic change in their diet can lead to stomach upsets, which can mean you end up with a very sick goat and possibly high vets bills before your new pet has even settled in properly.

Horns

Okay this isn't really a question but you should be aware that although you may think an Anglo Nubian Goat – or any goat really - looks lovely with horns these can be dangerous for you as an owner and your family as well as other pets that you may have and even to the goat itself. You may decide you like horns but just be aware that a goat with horns charging at full pelt can cause a lot of damage. Personally I wouldn't risk it, especially in a household with children or other animals but of course the choice is yours and you will find it is a very controversial topic amongst goat owners. Before buying you may want to ask the breeder if their goats are polled – which means naturally hornless – or whether they have their goats disbudded – which means removing the buds on the babies before they can grow into horns (See Chapter 9).

What has the worming procedure and general maintenance been? Again, to keep the care consistent and make the transition between the place they were born and your home as easy as possible for your new pets it is important you know how the goats have been raised. Ask any questions you can think of relating to the general maintenance of your new goats.

Have any of your goats died for unexplained reasons? This may be an uncomfortable question to ask but it is an important one because if the answer is yes then it may not be wise to buy from that breeder. Of course not all breeders will tell the truth but if you are asking in person you may be able to tell if they are lying or not.

Can I contact other buyers for references or speak with the herds' vet? Some breeders may say no and I'm not suggesting that those who do are bad sellers that are selling dodgy animals; some may refuse purely because they have a confidentiality policy and don't like passing on clients' details and this is perfectly fine. However, very good breeders should have some testimonials on their website or social media pages and you may be able to contact previous buyers this way. If not the breeder should at least be willing to give you their vet's contact details so that you can, if you wish to do so, contact them and ask about the health of the goats.

Extras

You may just want a general Anglo Nubian Goat to keep as a pet and not really care what it looks like as long as it's healthy. This is the stance I would take, as I believe that animals that are bred to have certain traits can also end up having medical problems but if you have seen one with unusual characteristics that appeal to you then this may be something you want to enquire about when approaching breeders however it may make it more difficult for you to find someone in your area.

Remember – DON'T BE AFRAID TO SAY NO!

You may travel for miles to see a goat that you are interested in purchasing but if you are unsure then don't feel pressurized into buying. You may be desperate for a pet goat (well two!) but always walk away if you have alarm bells ringing. There are plenty more sellers even if you have to wait a while longer or spend a bit more money it is worth it if it means you are getting a healthier animal that is better suited to you and your home.

As it can be disappointing to travel a long way only to find that the goats aren't what you were expecting, I would recommend you email a few breeders first, listing your questions and asking for photographs and proof of health testing and registration first so that you can be reassured that the breeder(s) you do visit are more than likely going to have suitable, healthy goats. From their replies you may also build up a rapport and find one that you think is more trustworthy just from the way they converse with you and how helpful they are.

Red Flags

Whilst it may be difficult to know if someone is telling the truth or not, if you come across any of the following from a seller you should go elsewhere:

- Lack of medical records especially the results of tests for CAE, CL and Johnes.
- A reluctance to send pictures or only sending one or two from the same angle.
- Lack of paperwork or unwillingness to send it. Someone giving lots of excuses as to why it isn't ready could be an indicator that the paperwork doesn't exist.
- Lack of information about the goats' parentage.
- Poor living conditions; too many goats and not enough land is usually an indicator of a bad seller, as is huge amounts of faeces and if the goats are living in unsuitable conditions from birth, chances are they will have health problems.
- Unhealthy looking goats - this is another reason why it is important to see a goat before purchasing it. If you can see the other goats in the herd it was born into you can see for yourself whether they look healthy or not. Don't buy a goat because you feel sorry for it, again, if it looks unhealthy it probably is.

Signs Of A Healthy Goat

Whilst it can be difficult to determine whether an animal is healthy unless you are a qualified vet, there are some signs you can look for to reduce the chances of buying a sick goat.

You should try to assess the following:

- Eyes – these should be bright and not dull or sick looking.
- Hooves – these should be properly trimmed, as overgrown feet can cause leg problems in the future as well as conditions such as Foot Rot (see Chapter 7 – Common Illnesses).
- Coat – this should be smooth and glossy with no lumps or cuts.
- Skin – this should be pliable and clean. There should be no lumps or bumps, as these could signal abscesses, which are highly contagious.
- Body – You should be able to feel the goats' ribs under their skin but their bones shouldn't jut out.

- Tail – this should be upright or relaxed not tucked in.
- Knees – should be smooth not knobbly, as knobbly knees can often be an indicator of CAE.
- Stance – the goats should look relaxed and not be hunched up.
- Feces/manure – not the nicest thing to study but you should check when you visit a herd that any droppings you see are firm, slightly moist pellets or balls rather than clumpy piles or runny messes. Check coloring too, as very dark feces may be this color because they contain blood. You could look online beforehand to get an idea of what healthy feces for these animals looks like.
- Urine – you may not see the goat urinate but if you do you should take note of whether it does so easily and without any effort or signs of pain.
- Personality – as mentioned previously, goats are all different, but generally if you are looking for a pet, choose one that is friendly rather than extremely shy or aggressive.

There may be other things that have not been mentioned above and it may be worth looking at photographs of healthy and unhealthy goats to give you an idea of what to look for when searching for one to buy.

Other Considerations

There may be other considerations aside from health and appearance to factor in depending on why you are buying a goat.

Family Pet

As you are reading this book, you clearly want an Anglo Nubian Goat as a pet. Therefore you should choose a doe or wether that is free of any major defects or health problems and whether they have a steep rump or incorrect breed character shouldn't matter to you. Really you just want to make sure that they have a friendly personality and will suit you and your family.

With this in mind I would try to choose a goat that was bottle fed as a kid as these tend to be friendlier towards humans than those that were raised by their mothers. Secondly I would get one without horns, as mentioned above these are just too dangerous to have as a family pet so look for either a naturally polled goat or one that has been disbudded at a young age (see Chapter 9).

Milk Provider
If you also want a pet that provides milk then you will be looking for something slightly different. For instance, clearly you want a female that is either pregnant or just had a baby, unless you are intending to breed her yourself. Despite what some people believe only females provide milk and only when they have been bred. Secondly, you will want one that is friendly, gentle, easy to milk and co-operative, especially if you have no experience. Thirdly, you will need to check that she has the correct sized teats and a good, strong udder attachment as a saggy, baggy udder can easily be damaged and can also be too low to get a bucket under.

For goats that will be milked, you should check that the female has not got any defects that will make birthing complicated. Whilst she doesn't have to be show quality, some faults could hinder kidding and/or milk production, for instance, bad feet or weak posterns could lead to difficulties with walking and eating in the future. To continually get milk from your female you will need to continue to breed her each year.

Lastly, you should check that your goat comes from a family that has a history of providing good quality milk in fairly high quantities.

The only problem with wanting to milk a goat that you are keeping as a pet is that you will have to breed your female goat each year and this can eventually take a toll on her body. You could buy two females and alternate which one you breed to give them chance to recover in between.

Show Pet
You may decide that you don't want a pet that you can milk but that you do want one to enter in shows or breed. If this is the case then you need to not only check for good general health but you will also need to purchase a registered goat that comes complete with papers.

A show standard goat also needs to be as close to 'ideal' as possible. This means no faults such as winged shoulders, bad feet, weak posterns, steep rumps and so on which means it will be more costly to purchase than one that isn't up to show standard.

Remember if you buy a cheaper goat that isn't an 'ideal' show standard you could still enter them in shows but it would be as part of the pet section rather than the purebred one.

Where To Buy

There are a variety of places where you can purchase an Anglo Nubian Goat and whilst I won't recommend one over the other – just like there are good and bad pet stores there are good and bad auctions, good and bad breeders and good and bad owners – I will try to list both the advantages and disadvantages of each. Often where you buy depends on the area in which you live, for instance, the only place reachable to you may be an auction or you may only have breeders available in your area.

As mentioned before, do your research; just because you know of one breeder in your area don't settle for them but look for others too, even if they are further afield, just in case you decide the nearest breeders' goats aren't of a high standard.

Auction

This may seem the most obvious and therefore the best place to purchase a goat from. This is because when most people think of goats they associate them with farms and therefore with animal auctions.

However, auctions are not always advisable because you won't be able to find out the history of the animals and those bought at auctions may already have illnesses or other problems that you won't know about until after you've purchased. This can be expensive if you end up paying for unexpected vet's bills but if you have other animals on your land already it can be catastrophic.

If you are going to purchase from an auction I would recommend that you ask about to see if you can find anyone who purchased from there in the past and find out what their experiences were like.

Local Shows

This is a good starting point to search for a goat, especially if you have the intention to breed. You can quickly build up a herd just by owning a couple of female goats and hiring a stud for mating. Of course you may not want to breed your goats if you are just keeping them for pets but local shows will give you the opportunity to study those that are considered 'good' specimens and listen to the judges' explanations as to why one placed higher than the other. Whilst this may not interest you (unless you want to enter your new pet into shows) visiting local shows is a great way to meet both owners and breeders and make contact with the local goat community. Many will be happy to discuss their animals, provide advice and tell stories about the joys of owning a goat as well as recommending breeders if they don't have any for sale themselves.

You never know, you may come across a reputable breeder that has goats already for sale and if you get to know them beforehand they may even do you a deal.

Local Breeders

It is always a good idea to find and visit a few breeders so you can compare the animals and their living conditions as well as the breeders themselves.

Of course, you may not have a lot nearby, in which case I would suggest speaking to several via email and telephone before you choose which one to visit. Ask the questions mentioned earlier and any others you may have. A responsible breeder will be only too happy to provide photographs and information about the kids that are for sale and their parents even if you haven't decided to purchase from them yet.

Make sure you explain exactly what you are looking for in a goat and explain the living arrangements you will have for your potential new pets, for instance the amount of land available, the type of fencing you have in place as well as how you intend to house your goats, whether you have other animals on your property and if so what kind, as well as mentioning if you have children or not. This will all help the breeder to match up the goats with you and your lifestyle so you can be confident they will have a suitable one available when you visit.

If they provide you with advice then take this on board, as it is a sign that they are concerned about their goats and who they sell them to. For instance, a breeder may tell you that you don't have enough space or suggest that you build your barn first or do more research before purchasing. I doubt very much that one would refuse to sell you a goat – unless you are adamant you are only going to keep one rather than a pair or they're really concerned about the goats' welfare with you - but if they do I would listen to their reasons why rather than getting angry and blaming them as a breeder.

Owners

As mentioned before you can buy goats on pre-loved or pre-owned websites. Usually these are people who have owned a goat but then their circumstances have changed, for instance, they may have moved and are looking to re-home their goats because they are not allowed to keep them on their new property. Other times people have kept goats as pets but have bred them either accidentally or so that they could have milk; if they decide to keep the female kids they may look to sell on their buck. Just be aware that if this is the case then you will be buying an intact buck and therefore you may want to get them neutered, for the reasons given previously, which will cost more money.

Whilst you can drop on lucky and get a goat for a cheap price on these websites you should still visit in person to check the goats' health and ask for proof of medical testing for Johnes Disease, CAE, etc.

Some people will put goats on these selling websites stating that you could register them and if they are kids then this may be true but if you want a registered goat make sure that you can do this before you buy. Often these people have bred their goats for milk and just want to sell the kids cheaply because they want to see them go to good homes rather than be killed for meat.

One final thought on buying from an owner rather than a breeder is that if you are a first time goat owner you will need to purchase two goats and it is easier to buy two from the same herd rather than from separate herds. This is because if they have come from separate herds they may take a dislike to each other or one will try to show dominance over the other whereas two that have been raised together from day one are more likely to get along. Some people will sell two or more goats; usually when they've just bred their female for milk and just want to get rid of the babies but if there is only one for sale I would probably not buy it unless you already have at least one or two goats already and are just looking to expand your herd.

Chapter 4: Feeding

If you look at the Internet for information about feeding Anglo Nubian Goats you will find that there is very little available and what there is can be scattered about over hundreds of different pages. When you do find any it is often conflicting information, which can be quite confusing.

Don't let this lack of information put you off. Feeding goats is fairly simple; they are herbivores and therefore eat plant-based foods. If you understand how their digestive system works then providing them with a suitable diet is far less scary.

How Does A Goat's Stomach Work?

Goats are classified as ruminants, meaning that instead of having one compartment in their stomach like we humans do, they have four. As the plant material is eaten, it travels through each chamber in turn and the nutrients are extracted.

The first three compartments contain tiny microorganisms, which break down the food that the goat eats. These microbes are actually living creatures and as such need to be kept healthy in order to keep your goat healthy. These microbes can be upset if the goat's diet is changed suddenly, which is why you should always introduce new foods slowly.

If you have ever watched a goat eat you may notice that sometimes they appear to inhale their food rather than chew it slowly. This rapidly consumed food is stored in the first and largest of the four chambers known as the rumen. This food will later be regurgitated and chewed at a more leisurely pace known as 'chewing the cud' or 'ruminating'.

As disgusting as this may sound to us it is important your goat does this, as it assists the microorganisms in breaking down the fibrous material and extract the nutrients. Once food reaches the final chamber – the abomasum – it is then processed in the same way as it would be in a single stomached animal.

What To Feed

Hay
Goats are designed to process fibrous plant material and therefore hay and plants should comprise the main bulk of their diet.

There are two main types of hay; leguminous hay such as alfalfa, and clover and non-leguminous hay made from green crops like barley and oats.

The former have higher protein levels and will contain more calcium. Non-leguminous hay is often thought to be inferior and less palatable, however it can be rich in carbohydrates. A good compromise therefore is a mix of high quality leguminous and grass hay.

Depending on the nutrient level, a typical adult will eat around five pounds of grass hay a day, if not more.

Only use high quality hay that has been stored correctly. Moldy hay cannot only make your goat sick but is also a fire hazard.

Hay should be available all the time, even for those goats that forage all day.
Goats are notorious for picking out the tastiest pieces of food and throwing the rest away, so it is often more economical to use feeders that are designed to prevent this waste. These feeders usually have bars spaced 4-5 inches apart, which allows the goat to reach the hay but prevents them from sticking their head in to pull it all out.

Another popular option is hay bags however many people don't like these because there are many horror stories circulating about goats becoming entangled and strangling themselves. If you do prefer to use one then my advice would be to only do so if you are around to constantly supervise your goat when they're using it.

Foraging
It is a myth that goats will eat tin cans and trampolines and anything else they happen across, so don't worry too much if you leave a lawn

chair or two out. It is also a misconception that goats will eat the whole of your lawn so that you will no longer have to mow it. They are browsers rather than grazers and whilst they may indeed eat patches of your lawn they will not eat the whole thing all in one go. They tend to be opportunistic feeders, meaning that if they happen along your prized pansies during a foraging session they will most likely snap them up rather than eat your lawn, so keep this in mind when you are allowing them free roam of your garden. However, they are not picky, so whether it is a freshly grown sapling they find or a pile of weeds they will eat it.

It is important to allow access to natural outside vegetation that they can forage themselves, as this provides them with exercise and also reduces the amount of hay you need to feed them. The advantage of keeping these animals as pets is that plants we consider weeds will make a tasty meal for them, so whilst you may still need to mow your lawn once in a while, you shouldn't have to pull up too many weeds anymore!

To prevent damaging their rumens or developing an overeating disease known as Enterotoxemia, different vegetation should be introduced slowly to your goat every spring.

Toxic Plants
Before letting your goat(s) roam free and eat whatever they like, you should be aware of what plants are growing in their outdoor enclosure, as some plants can be extremely poisonous to goats.

Plants such as Azaleas, Hemlock, Rhubarb, Mountain Laurel and Rhododendrons are all extremely toxic and should be removed from any area that the goat is going to be let loose in, so make sure you do a thorough check of your garden, preferably before your goat comes to live with you.

There is a long list of plants that are toxic to goats available on the Internet and there's far too many for me to list in this book. Not only that, but the list is constantly changing as people post that a certain plant isn't toxic whilst a new one may appear on the list, so for the most up to date information it is better to do a quick Google search.

Not only is it impractical for me to list them all here it is also near impossible to remove them all from any garden, especially if you have a lot of land. The guidance therefore is to find the ones that are the most toxic and remove those and make sure there is plenty of other vegetation for them to choose from. Usually if a goat has access to plenty of non-toxic plants, they will usually avoid (or at least just have a nibble) on those that are mildly toxic to them, which means they shouldn't get ill.

What If There Aren't Many Plants To Forage?
If you don't have access to a pasture and your goat is being kept in a small enclosure that doesn't have many plants available or your goat eats them too quickly for them to grow back, you can go out and forage plants for them yourself and scatter them about in your back garden. Plants that are good include dandelion, nettles, kale, thistle, multiflora rose, thistle and chicory. They also like sweet corn husks and stalks, carrots, kale, turnips, pumpkins and beets. Just ensure that the plants you give them are free from pesticides and other potentially harmful chemicals, if you are foraging from surrounding land you may want to give food a good wash first before feeding.

Another idea, depending on how much land you have available, would be to section off part of your garden from your goats where you can grow plants for their food. This way they can't get to them before they're fully-grown and you can be absolutely certain that they are safe for your goat and free from chemicals.

Minerals
Goats need vitamins and minerals to keep healthy. Some of this they will receive from their hay, but this alone isn't enough to supply them with all the vitamins and minerals they need. Even the amount found in hay can vary depending on where it is grown, therefore it is recommended to feed them a separate mineral to prevent vitamin and mineral deficiencies.

When buying goat mineral, look for one that includes both calcium and phosphorous, as these two minerals are necessary to build healthy, strong bones and helps females make milk.

The ratio is very important and should be 2:1, which means two parts calcium to one part phosphorous. Often ten percent calcium to eight percent phosphorous is a common way to see it listed.

Mineral mix should also contain salt. Vitamins A, D and E are often added, as is Ammonium Chloride, which helps prevent urinary calculi, common in male goats. Most will also have small amounts of copper, zinc, magnesium, potassium, manganese and selenium.

Water

All living creatures need access to fresh water in order to thrive and Anglo Nubian Goats are no different. In fact, they need plenty of water in order to keep their rumens in good working order. For males, water can help prevent urinary calculi and keep their urinary tracts healthy and as goat's milk is mainly comprised of water, it is especially important if you have lactating does.

Some goats can be very particular and some owners report that their goat will refuse to drink because there is a bit of dirt in the water or because it didn't taste right to them, so ensure it is always clean and fresh and change it periodically throughout the day.

If you find your goat doesn't seem to be drinking much water, especially in the winter months, try giving them warm water, as they seem to enjoy this more than icy cold, so warming their water slightly can increase their intake.

In the summer months, you may find they are drinking more because of the sunshine. If you have extremely hot weather it may be a good idea to put ice mixed with water in buckets around the goats' enclosure or in their water trough. This will eventually melt, ensuring your goats always have access to fresh water. This is particularly important if you are out during the day for long periods.

Any does that you are milking or that are nursing will need to replenish the water they have lost in providing milk, so always make sure there is plenty of water available after you have finished milking and throughout the day.

Clean water is the cheapest, yet most important nutrient in your goats' diet so make sure that there is always a generous supply available and easily accessible to them.

Grain

If you are giving grain, this should only comprise around ten percent of a goat's diet. However, it is worth noting that there are mixed opinions with regards to grain. Some owners say that their goats become moody and describe them as "spoilt brats" when they get grain whilst others say that a small amount is fine. Goats don't need grain to survive and they will live happily on pasture, hay or a combination of both but for pregnant or lactating does, growing kids and bucks in rut it can be a good, quick source of energy. It is also believed that grain can help keep their body heat up when it's cold at night, so if you are in an area that is incredibly cold you may want to consider feeding grain in the winter.

It is thought that feeding grain can improve milk quality, so it is a good way to provide extra vitamins, minerals and proteins for pregnant or lactating does.

However, grain can cause weight gain, bloating and digestive upsets if too much is fed, so only feed in moderation and don't overdo it. For pregnant does, half a cup of grain will suffice and can be increased to one cup a hundred days into their pregnancy and while ever they're being milked.

For kids and rutting or breeding males, a quarter to half a cup of grain per day should be enough.

Adult males that aren't being bred and wethers shouldn't be given grain, as it can increase the chances of urinary calculi.

Scraps And Treats

A question many people ask me is 'do you feed your goat leftover scraps from your kitchen?' The answer is yes. There's no reason why you can't do this as long as you remember that goats are herbivores and therefore only eat plant based foods, so don't go giving them a Sunday roast covered in gravy!

Fruit and vegetables are perfectly fine and you will find that your goat will love orange, apples and bananas – peel and all.

Many people worry that different foods will change the flavor of their goats' milk and certain plants such as chamomile and daisies can make the milk taste bad.

Other treats include carrots, raisins, sunflower seeds, pumpkin and pumpkin seeds and greens.

Remember these scraps and treats should only be fed in moderation and, as mentioned above, introduced individually and very slowly into their diet so as not to upset your goats' stomachs.

Store Bought Goat Feed
Stores will try to promote goat feed and new owners will often buy it thinking it is something their Anglo Nubian Goat needs. Unfortunately, what they don't realize is that most of these feeds are comprised of grain. The owners unwittingly feed their goats this and because they can't really handle more than ten percent of grain in their diet they quickly become ill. This is because a high amount of grain produces acidosis, which is an imbalance of acid in their bodies. As goats are meant to be more alkaline than acid, they get very sick and experience pain, bloating, constipation, skin problems and it can lead to death.

If you do purchase goat feed then read the bag carefully and only give it in very small amounts alongside hay and foraged foods.

You can save money by purchasing food for cattle as this is often cheaper than those aimed at goats. Avoid sheep mix as although it shouldn't make them ill goats need a higher level of copper than sheep and so you may find that if you give your Anglo Nubian sheep mix you will have to supplement them with a copper mineral otherwise their levels will drop to low which can eventually lead to poor health.

Supplements

Other than the minerals mentioned above, goats don't really need any added supplements. You can boost a goat's health if necessary, so it is sometimes helpful to keep a stock of the following:

- Black Oil Sunflower Seeds – These make a great treat for your goat and can be bought from pet stores or anywhere else that sells goat feed. They will give your goat a shiny coat and healthy skin. For lactating goats you can add a little into their grain mixture after milking.
- Probiotics – This helps poor rumen function, however you shouldn't give it to your goats all the time, as it's just not necessary. If your goat is getting over a major illness or is coming to the end of a course of antibiotics then probiotics may help them, however always make sure you use one specifically for ruminant animals otherwise you could end up doing more harm than good.
- Baking Soda – You can pick this up from your local supermarket and it is great for stomach upsets or bloating, as it can help rebalance the PH in their rumens. If you do suspect bloating or digestive problems it is always wise to consult a vet first before administering this supplement.
- Herbal De-wormer Mix – This should be given every six months in order to de-worm your goats and keep them healthy.

Points To Remember

Goats can easily become bored of your lawn and move onto weeds, rose bushes and trees – both the bark and the leaves – so make sure they have a good variety of foods. If you have particular plants you are precious about and don't want your goats to eat them, ensure these are far away from your goats' enclosure.

A nutritious diet equals healthier goats. Although you are probably only thinking of buying a couple of goats to keep as pets, you may eventually decide that you would like to breed your animals or have them provide milk, so it is worth noting here that there have been studies that have shown a direct correlation between a high quality diet and increased fertility and healthier kids as well as an increase in birth weight.

Remember to keep your goats' diet simple; a variety of green plants; foraged, hay and pasture – with the odd vegetable treat now and then is enough to keep your goats happy. Keep grains to a minimum and avoid tin cans and other junk and you and your goat should be happy.

Always check the calcium and phosphorous levels in any grain, store bought feed, minerals and supplements you are giving to ensure they are balanced in your goats' diet, too much or too little of either or both can lead to your goat becoming ill.

Chapter 5: Fencing And Housing

If you ask somebody who owns goats how you can tell if your fence is good enough to keep your goats safe you may get the reply "throw a bucket of water at it, if the water can get through then so can your goats." This is a popular saying that highlights the fact that goats can pretty much get out of anything if they have the mind to do so.

One mistake many first time goat owners make is they assume that a fence is a fence and as long as there are no holes in it then their existing one should be fine. My advice is not to underestimate them; you may not be able to see an obvious way out but that doesn't mean your goats won't find one!

You may be lucky and end up with a couple that aren't interested in escaping but most goats will try to jump over, crawl under, climb or stand on, lean against or squeeze through pretty much any boundary they come across, so I would strongly recommend that you invest in a good fence from the very beginning to save time and money having to replace it later.

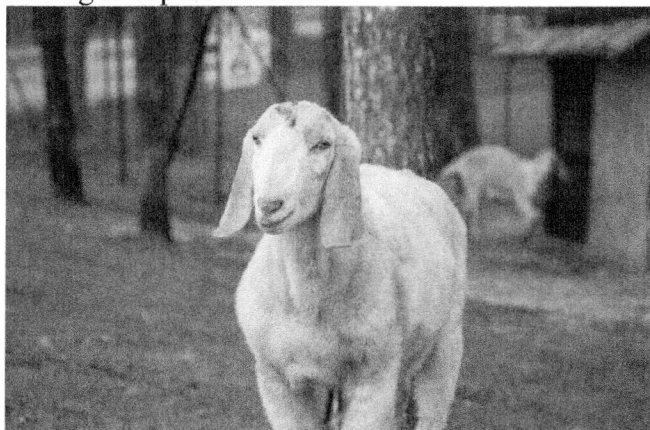

There are so many different options for goat fencing that it can be daunting. You need your fence to keep your goats enclosed but also to keep any predators out. It needs to be strong enough that it can't be knocked over easily or blown down by high winds. It also needs to be high enough that your goats can't jump or climb over it.

It may sound simple enough but these goats are very cunning escape artists and it is amazing to see them squeeze under a fence that you thought was impenetrable.

Many people will use cattle fencing but this can be quite flimsy so I would avoid this.

Another option is chain link but there are two drawbacks with this. Firstly it is possible to climb although they may find it difficult. Secondly goats have a tendency to push on the bottom of a fence to get to the grass on the other side and chain link often gives. As soon as your goats notice this they will push harder so unless the fence has been anchored at the bottom to something incredibly strong that won't give under pressure, eventually the links will separate. I'm not saying it will happen immediately but over time your goats may manage to get through a chain link fence. They will then devour anything tasty on the other side, which, if you're not on a large farm, will be your neighbors' garden. They're also at risk of being hurt by dogs and other predators so it really is in your best interest to keep your goats as safe as possible.

A third option is welded wire fencing, which are squares welded together. These squares will come in many different sizes and it tends to be one of the cheapest options, but many owners will say to avoid this because the goats will stand on and rub themselves along the fencing, which eventually causes the welds to break.

So what are your options for fencing?

You're really left with woven wire fencing or electric fencing.

Woven wire fencing is squares woven at the corners. Whilst these fences tend to be sturdy, they also tend to be the most expensive. However, as it will withstand more wear and tear it is often better to pay more upfront rather than having to constantly repair or replace it.

This type of fencing comes in different sized squares; usually 2x4 inches, 4x4 inches and 6x6 inches. The smaller the square the more costly the fence, which means you could be tempted to use 6x6 inches just to keep the cost down however make sure it is safe and the goats cannot get their heads through otherwise they could get stuck.

Your final option is electric fencing, which uses high tensile wire connected to a charger to electrify it. Up to seven strands is usually enough to suffice. These are fairly easy to install and can be fairly cheap in comparison to the woven wire fencing. If you train your goats to stay away from it, make sure your fence is always charged properly and ensure the bottom wire is kept away from grass or other plants so that it doesn't short out then it can be effective.

Whilst each option can work successfully alone the ideal would be a combination of woven wire fencing with electric strands at the top and the bottom. The electric strands at the bottom should be on the outside of the fence, as this will help keep predators out, whilst the strands at the top will keep your goats from jumping or climbing over it.

Goat fencing is confusing because there are a lot of options and there are a lot of ideas about what works and what doesn't because what works for one goat owner may not necessarily be suitable for another and it is dependent on how determined and curious your goats are and how big a property you have.

I am recommending a combination of woven wire and electric, because this is what works best for the majority of goat owners, but I think it is important to take into account the size and layout of your land. Electric fencing may not be suitable if you have other peoples' property connected to yours, especially if they own pets such as dogs and cats so always take this into consideration as well.

Whichever type of fencing you use it should be a minimum of five feet otherwise your goats may be able to jump over it.

Fence Posts
It can be very tempting to cut corners when you are building a fence but these are wily creatures and my advice is to follow the guidelines for fencing livestock when you are installing fence posts.

Make sure that your posts are sturdy and fixed correctly. A general rule of thumb is that when you are erecting a fence, one third of the height of the post should be fixed into the ground, so for a post that is 7-8 feet long, 2 – 2.5 feet of fence post should be in the ground. It is worth marking your posts before setting them in so that you don't put them in too deep and make your fence too short or not put them in deep enough and risk making your fence less sturdy.

Remember you will also need a few inches extra at the top, so if you are installing a six foot fence you will want six foot and a few inches of fence post sticking out of the ground in order to have enough room to securely attach the top of your fence.

The most tension will be on the corners and near the gate, so this is where you will want to install H-braces. You could also add diagonal wire bracing as well at these points so that it puts opposite tension on the fence, so the wire should be attached at the bottom of the corner post and run to the top of the H-brace attached to the next fence post.

Try to keep fence posts no more than ten feet apart for the main fence and no more than eight feet apart where your H-braces are located, as this will provide extra support. Whilst this rule works best, it does depend on the type of fence you use and the size of it, so do research and ask the people you are buying it from for their input too before installing.

One thing people do forget about is the soil that they are digging into. You may find that your posts are secure simply by digging a hole, putting the fence post in and shoveling the soil back around it but if you live in an area where the soils is soft or even sandy then this may not be enough and you may find that your posts start to wiggle and lean after a while. Pound your fence posts in as hard as you can and secure the posts with concrete if possible. Whilst this makes it more time consuming and expensive, it is better to have a secure fence then one that is going to fall over at the slightest touch (or head butt!).

Housing

Some people suggest that you build stalls in your goats' shelter in case one becomes ill or if you are planning to breed. This way you can segregate if necessary. It is far better to put these in at the beginning than further down the line, so think carefully when you are planning your goats' shed. However, don't think that your goat will be happy to sit in their own stall day in, day out. I would keep your goats together and only separate if one is ill, to provide a birthing stall if you are going to breed or when feeding if you want to ensure that both goats are getting the same amount of food. Goats are sociable and need companionship so should be allowed to roam about their enclosures, both inside and out, together.

Goats aren't that particular with their shelter, but when building one you should consider the following:

- Can **you** enter and exit the shelter easily? Remember you will need to do a routine clean and therefore it needs to be accessible for you as well as your goats.
- Will there be running water and electricity nearby? This will make it a whole lot easier when you are cleaning, feeding and watering your goats.
- Do you have room to put a store nearby for your goat feed, bedding, toys and other supplies? Again this just makes the care a lot easier. If you are alternating toys then you will need a shed big enough to keep these in when they're not in use.
- Can you insulate your enclosure? If you live in a warm climate then your goats may not have an issue with this, but if you live somewhere that gets very, very cold then you may need to consider insulating your shed or using heat pads. Anglo Nubian Goats are fairly good at adjusting to temperatures but your shelter needs to prevent draughts and keep them dry in wet conditions, as they can be susceptible to Pneumonia.
- Is there enough room to provide toys? Goats are very active and in wet weather they may be inside a lot but they still need to keep themselves occupied so you should try and put in a small climbing or play area such as little platforms made of pallets or crates.

Size

The size of your barn or shelter depends on how big you are planning your herd to be and of course how much land you have available. For Anglo Nubian Goats, the general rule is 200 square feet per goat. It can possibly be smaller if you live in a hot country where your goats will spend the majority of their time outside, but consider both winter and summer and whether they are likely to be in or out more in each season. For instance in the UK you will find that you will keep your goats indoors for the majority of the time, at least during winter and spring because it is rain. Goats do not like getting wet and it can lead to lots of health conditions. Therefore your indoor space would need to be large enough to accommodate both goats, feeding and water areas, bedding and sleeping areas and toys. Of course if they are indoors most of the time then the outdoor enclosure won't need to be as big, likewise if your goats are outdoors more, the outdoor enclosure needs to be big but the indoor shelter can be smaller.

One mistake many people make is looking at how much space they need and building the shelter with one goat in mind, not realizing that actually they need at least two of these animals. Always make sure you that you at least double your measurements.

The second mistake they make is not realizing how cute and addictive these pets can be and they build a shed big enough for two of these goats then further down the line decide they want three or more or they want to breed – their shed is no longer big enough and they end up having to pull it down and build a new one. If you think you will end up keeping more than two of these animals then build your shelter with this in mind. Even if you don't increase your herd your goats will be happy with the extra space. Of course you may not have a choice if you don't have acres and acres of land and you may only have enough space for two.

Please don't buy any goats if you have measured your back garden and found that you don't have enough room. The minimum size requirements are there for a reason; your goats will not be healthy or happy on a tiny bit of land.

A goat shelter doesn't have to be super expensive; if you are good with your hands (or know someone who is) then you can build it yourself out of new or recycled materials. As long as it is sturdy and practical with enough space and free from draughts it really doesn't matter what it's made from.

Flooring

This isn't something people often think about when they are considering purchasing goats, but it is important and you should consider the advantages and disadvantages of each option and decide which is better suited for you and your animals.

Wooden floors can be warm and dry but they can also absorb urine and have a tendency to rot.

Concrete is great because urine can't run off and you can simply wash it down with a hose. However, it does require frequent cleaning and as it can be cold in winter you will need thick bedding.

Earthen floor is your last option and is probably the easiest type with goats, as it is easy to maintain because excess urine drains away and it requires a lot less cleaning and bedding changes. As soil is warmer and more comfortable for goats than wood or concrete, you don't need to use as much bedding. Whilst you will need to do the occasional deep clean to keep bacteria levels and insects at bay, if you do daily spot checks these deep cleans can just be done once or twice a year if you have a soil floor.

Shade

You will need to provide your goat with shade to allow them to get out of the sun as well as an indoor shelter. This can be as simple as putting a table under a large tree or adding a platform with a ramp to the side of your barn so your goat can sit underneath for shade or climb on top to sit in the sun or play. If you do add some sort of shelter on the side of your indoor enclosure just remember that they may try to climb on the roof so ensure that everything is safe.

Supply Shed

This can again be built on the side of your goat shed or can be a completely separate building. It doesn't need to look amazing but it is helpful to have one nearby so that everything you need is to hand, making cleaning and taking care of your goats a lot easier.

The main things to include in your supply shed are:

- Goat feed, for instance, alfalfa pellets and grain. Keep them in waterproof and rodent/pest proof containers.
- Goat treats and supplements, such as sunflower seeds, baking soda and minerals.
- Straw for bedding.
- Leashes, brushes and hoof trimmers for general goat maintenance and care.
- General 'work bucket' to hold any supplies you may need whilst working in your goat area.
- If you are milking then you may want to keep any milking equipment in this shed too as well as wet wipes and antibacterial spray for cleaning udders before and after milking.
- You may also want to keep your medicines in this supplies shed too if you do decide to keep some in stock. This is entirely up to you, I know of people that keep it in their store shed and others that keep them inside their house and I think it is dependent on your own preference as well as what you are choosing to keep in stock and the temperatures they need to be stored at. Many pet owners don't bother storing medicines because it is easier to just consult the vet rather than try to diagnose and treat an illness by yourself.
- One suggestion I would make is to label up all your goat equipment so that you can find it easily when you need it. Whilst it is fine to just keep everything in their original packaging and throw it all in, you may get irritated when you're having to search through piles of stuff just to find a packet of sunflower seeds. I've seen a lot of lovely supply sheds where everything has been placed in glass jars or plastic storage containers and labeled so that the owner just has to put their hand in and pull out what they need.

I would also advise that you lock up your goat shed both for the safety of any young children that may be in your house and also to prevent your goats from helping themselves.

Chapter 6: Goat Toys

Many people who are considering purchasing goats don't even think about goat toys, rather they picture these cute little creatures standing around on their lawn gazing thoughtfully at the fence, nibbling the grass and weeds here and there. An idyllic image, but (and I can't stress this enough) your goat will not be happy just standing around in a field in your garden all day even with another goat or other farm animals for company, and trust me a bored goat is a naughty goat and your new pet will soon get into trouble climbing the fence and trying to escape.

Goats are very intelligent creatures and as such get bored very easily. The good news is you can keep your new friends happy simply by buying a few cheap items for them to play with. If you are handy with a hammer and nails you could make exciting toys for them. It doesn't have to look pretty; your goat won't care as long as it's functional and interesting for them to play with.

A few goat toy ideas include:
- Plastic or wooden children's playhouses – Your goat will love going in and out of these. One with ladders and slides will provide them with hours of entertainment, but you can easily attach a few planks to make ramps for them to climb up and down if you wish to do so. Be aware that brand new, these are often very expensive so I would recommend you buy second hand ones either via yard sales, car boot sales or on websites such as Gumtree, Craigslist, eBay or Facebook marketplace to name but a few.
- Large Rocks – Great for climbing. Arrange a few to make a 'rock playground' for your goat. The extra advantage of rocks is that they will help wear down their hooves, so you won't have to trim them as often.
- Pallets or plastic crates – Again, these can be great fun and you can either just stack them at various heights to make different sized platforms, put them together to make steps or keep them at similar heights and attach wooden planks between them to make bridges for your goats to walk from

one to another. Many large companies or builder's yards will give used pallets away for free.

- Large Tyres – For example tractor tires or large car tires are great toys for goats. Stand them upright and half bury them in the ground and your goats will jump up and stand on top. Put a few together so they can climb and jump from one to the other.
- Logs – These can be stacked into a pyramid to make a climbing toy or can be used to make ramps or bridges. Lay one down and attach a board to the top and you have a great seesaw.
- Wooden Cable Spools – These are great platforms for your goats to climb on and if you want to make it into a kind of climbing frame for your goats you can do so by attaching wooden logs or planks to make bridges, slides and ramps. Again, if you're lucky you may find them for free from electrical or DIY stores, energy and phone companies or even electricians.
- Furniture – many people put out old tables, benches and even sofas and chairs for their goats to play on. Basically anything a goat can climb on will make a good toy. If you have a tree in your garden, placing a table or bench underneath will not only provide a place for your goat to lay down in the shade but they will also be able to climb up to nibble the lower branches as well as having fun simply jumping on and off. If you don't have any old ones of your own you can buy second hand or even make your own from any wood you have lying about.
- Scratching Post – You can make these very cheap by buying a few scrubbing brushes and nailing them either onto a fence post or any large post set into the ground. Your goats will have great fun scratching their backs and heads on them.
- Tether Ball – If you're in the UK then you may be more familiar with the term 'swing ball' but basically fix a large post in the ground and attach a ball to it with sturdy rope. Your goats will love head butting the ball to make it swing around.
- Small Trampolines – goats will love to jump on and off these and may even have a nap or two on them.

- Plastic Tunnels – Small goats love running through tunnels. You can combine them with platforms and pallets to make a great obstacle course for your new pets.
- Other goat toy ideas are baby rattles attached to the fence, plastic children's slides, plastic barrels and empty children's paddling pools or sandboxes.

Goats are great jumpers and climbers, which makes them incredibly fun to watch whilst they explore and play with their new toys. Just keep this in mind when setting up your goat playground and always keep climbing toys in the center of their fenced area because otherwise you may find they use their new platforms as a means of jumping over the fence!

If you only have a small garden then this may limit what you can provide for your goat, however you can alternate toys on a weekly or fortnightly basis and this may prevent your goat from becoming bored, as they will always have a variety of different things to keep them interested.

Always make sure the items you use are sturdy and 'goat proof', that is never give them anything they can destroy in a few minutes. You may need to replace items over time but things like wooden pallets, logs and plastic crates should be fairly sturdy and long lasting. Your goat may have a chew on some of their toys, although they tend to prefer wood and natural items to plastic however if you are feeding them properly then they shouldn't eat things like tires and hoses.

Do a quick online search for goat toys and you will find plenty of good photographs online to give you an idea of how to stack pallets or make bridges and platforms to keep your goats happy and occupied for years to come.

Lastly, remember you can pick up many of these items cheaply or for free. Don't be afraid to approach large companies and ask them if they reuse or recycle their pallets and wooden cable spools or if you can have them, the worst they can say is no but you will find that many don't have the storage space to keep them and they'll most likely be glad for you to take them off their hands.

Chapter 7: Common Illnesses

Like any living creature, goats are susceptible to a variety of illnesses. The good news is many of them are preventable as long as you understand how to correctly take care of your goat and provide them with suitable living conditions and a healthy, varied diet.

There may be other conditions not listed here that affect Anglo Nubian Goats but for the purpose of this book I've listed the most common ones. It is intended to be used as a guide only and to help you spot any signs of illness; if you are worried at any time about your goat's health then the best way to diagnose would be to consult a vet.

Enterotoxaemia
This is also known as the overeating disease and is caused by… overeating. When the balance of bacteria in their rumens is disrupted, a certain bacteria produces a poison that multiplies rapidly and makes the goat ill.

Symptoms
Symptoms include teeth grinding, high temperature or fever, diarrhea, sudden appetite loss, a swollen stomach or stomach pain which may result in the goat kicking their stomach, staggering about, crying out or lying on their side or looking depressed. Eventually they will be unable to stand and will lie on their side making paddling movements.

How To Treat
There is no effective cure and usually Enterotoxaemia is fatal. The only thing you can do is to consult your vet, who may advise you euthanize your goat if there is nothing they can do.

Prevention
This is definitely a case of prevention is better than cure and the good news is you can avoid this disease completely. Introduce new foods slowly and don't allow too many treats. Lock up your feed store and make sure your goat cannot get into it at all. Feeding in

two halves twice daily and giving hay as free choice can reduce over feeding.

In some countries such as the US there is a vaccination that can prevent overeating, so if you have a particularly greedy goat you may want to consider this, but if you only have a couple of goats as backyard pets and you keep them in a dry area and don't over feed you can easily prevent this.

Worms
These are internal parasites that suck the blood of the goat, internally weakening their immune system, which then makes them susceptible to other illnesses such as Pneumonia. If left untreated, a goat can eventually die, either from the worms themselves or from contracting a secondary illness. If your goat seems off, the best thing to do first is to check for worms.

Symptoms
Symptoms include a dull coat, loss of appetite, pale gums, diarrhea or stools that are clumped together, weight loss, lethargy and for lactating does, a drop in milk production.

The best way to get a diagnosis is to send a feces sample to a vet, but if you want to do a quick check at home then gently pull out the lower eyelid and check its color. Worms suck the blood of the goat and therefore cause anaemia, which is a low red blood cell count. Your goat's eyelids should be a rich salmon color or bright pink. If it is pale pink or white then your goat probably has worms.

Treatment
The first thing to do is to de-worm your goat. Many people prefer to use organic de-worming products and whilst I can understand this I feel that if your goat already has a large number of worms that are making them sick then a chemical de-wormer usually works quicker. Usually, with a chemical de-wormer you should give a second dose after eleven days in case there were any eggs missed during the first dose that will then have grown into adult worms.

As well as giving the de-wormer, provide a course of probiotics to help restore the natural balance to their rumens and start giving iron supplements until the red blood cell count is restored.

You may also want to consult a vet, as they will be able to recommend the best products to use.

Prevention
A goat will always have a number of worms inside them, there's not really any way to prevent them. However, when the numbers become very high it will start to make your goat sick. To keep the numbers low you have a choice as to whether to use a chemical de-wormer or an organic one made from herbs.

A chemical de-wormer is usually given twice a year, although many people will say to rotate which ones you use because otherwise the worms can build up immunity. (If you do switch don't just change the brand, check the label to make sure the chemicals are different, as you will find that many popular brands will contain the same ingredients).

If you are milking your goat then you will need to toss the milk after giving them a chemical de-wormer, as it isn't safe to drink for a week. Many chemical de-wormers aren't suitable for pregnant goats either, so always check the label.

A natural de-wormer is usually administered once a week to once a month.
A herbal de-wormer doesn't affect the milk at all, so is a better option for pregnant or lactating does.

Feeding your goats hay and pumpkin is another way to keep worms at bay.

Having feeding equipment suspended from the ground so feces cannot fall into it and cleaning your barn and garden on a regular basis can also prevent an infestation of worms.

For anyone who has a large amount of land for their goats then practicing controlled grazing by giving them different parts of the pasture for them to graze on. However for goats who are kept as back garden pets this isn't always possible therefore you should try to bring in foraged foods for them so they have new things to graze on rather than the same bit of land as this can help reduce the number of worms they pick up as well.

Pneumonia
Pneumonia is the inflammation or infection of the lungs and is used to describe a range of respiratory infections. It can quickly kill goats, especially young kids.

Symptoms
There are many symptoms of Pneumonia such as refusing food, hanging their heads, rapid, shallow or labored breathing signalled by their sides heaving. You may notice that your goat is listless, has a runny nose or nasal discharge. Sometimes your goat will sound congested or you may hear their chest rattling. Your goat will also develop a high fever. Pneumonia will eventually lead to death if left untreated.

How To Treat
If you suspect one of your goats has Pneumonia then you need to isolate them from the others immediately to stop it from spreading. To reduce the fever you should hydrate your goat. Antibacterial drugs such as Oxytetracycline can help but I would always seek advice from a qualified vet as well because a goat's lungs can rapidly fill up with fluid, which can quickly kill them.

Prevention
Goats of any breed are highly susceptible to this disease, however the chances of them actually becoming ill with Pneumonia is generally low as long as their housing is well ventilated and free from draughts.

If you live in a particularly cold area then you may want to consider putting heat pads in your barn to keep your goats warm during winter.

Acidosis

This is when a goat's rumen PH becomes acidic and can occur if they accidentally ingest a high amount of concentrated food stuff like grain.

Symptoms

The goat may stagger about or have muscle twitching, hang their head or stare off into space for long period of time. Teeth grinding, bloating and swelling of the left flank are also symptoms of Acidosis.

Treatment

Try to neutralize the acid in their rumens by giving them something alkaline such as bicarbonate of soda. Stop access to food and provide them with smaller portions so that their rumens have time to rebalance.

As always, contact the vet to get advice.

Prevention

Acidosis is easy to avoid simply by providing a well-balanced diet that includes lots of hay as well as not overfeeding and not giving too much grain. Lock up your grain and food stores so that your goats cannot help themselves whenever they feel like it. Keep an eye on their intake of fresh spring grass if you have large pastures.

In addition, avoid sudden diet changes that may upset your goats' rumen and provide plenty of long stemmed fiber to keep their digestive tract healthy.

Caprine Arthritis Encephalitis (CAE)

This is a contagious viral disease and the main way it spreads is from mother to baby via colostrum or milk. It may also be spread amongst adult goats via bodily fluids or feces if a goat is already infected.

Although it doesn't appear that CAE can be passed to humans, some countries will still need you to report any cases of this to the relevant authorities, so you should check the guidance on this online if your goat has contracted it. I believe it probably only affects those who are supplying goats milk to the general public, but it is always better to make sure just to be on the safe side.

There are five main forms of CAE: Arthritis, Pneumonia, Mastitis, Encephalitis and Chronic Wasting.

Symptoms

Arthritic CAE – Symptoms include poor hair condition, reluctance to rise and/or walk, stiffness or swollen joints, weight loss, abnormal posture and sudden lameness. As the disease progresses you may notice your goat start to walk on their knees. Arthritic CAE is mostly seen in adults aged one to two years.

Pneumonic CAE – Symptoms include a chronic cough, weight loss and difficulty breathing.

Mastitic CAE – This only affects pregnant or lactating does and symptoms include decreased milk production coupled with a hard, swollen udder.

Encephalitic – Lack of co-ordination, head tilt, blindness, depression, seizures, progressive paralysis and eventually death. This type of CAE is usually seen in kids of around two to four months old.

Chronic Wasting – This can be symptomatic of all types of CAE listed above. This is where the goat continues to lose weight even though there is no apparent loss of appetite.

Treatment
Whatever form it takes, CAE is a painful disease and unfortunately there is no specific treatment. Goats that contract this disease can be given care to support their condition such as pain medication and antibiotics to treat any bacterial infections that develop as a result, but there is no known cure as such. Usually the kindest thing to do with Encephalitic CAE is to euthanize your goat, as no matter how much care is provided your goat will suffer and eventually die.

If you believe your goat is suffering from CAE then always contact a vet for advice.

Quarantine the infected goat and if any kids were nursing, stop this immediately to prevent it spreading.

Prevention
As you are most likely just buying a couple of goats as pets, prevention is far better than ending up with high vet bills and sick animals. To avoid bringing CAE onto your land you simply have to check that the goats you intend to purchase are free from CAE, so always ask the breeder or owner before you buy. Anyone who is genuine will be happy to provide the results of the tests. However, make sure you don't just check the results for the goats you have purchased but for the whole herd. Personally, I would want to see that all animals from this seller had been free for at least a year or two just to be on the safe side. Don't be afraid to ask if they have ever had any cases of CAE. It is definitely better to buy from someone who can explain about this disease rather than from someone who acts dumb about it or who genuinely hasn't heard of it.

Do not purchase a goat unless you are satisfied that a CAE test has been done and all the animals in the herd have had negative results.

A CAE test is a simple blood test and is relatively cheap so if you are in doubt, get a test done yourself via your vet.

If you have never had goats on your land before and those you purchase are CAE free, then you should never have to worry about this if you are just keeping a couple as pets. Just remember that if one of your goats dies and you replace it or if you decide to breed or add to your herd, then you should only introduce new goats onto your land if you have done a test. Any babies that are born should also be tested just to rule out any new genetic introductions that may have arisen.

Caseous Lymphadentitis (CL)

This is a disease caused by bacteria that results in abscesses, which can be both external and internal and can eventually spread to the lungs and digestive tract.

It is highly contagious and is spread when an abscess bursts and another goat comes into contact with the pus.

Symptoms

Usually you will notice abscesses around the mouth or jaw, shoulder, neck, knees or upper leg.

If a goat has internal abscesses then you may notice excessive coughing.

Eventually, the abscess will burst by itself, which is when it can be dangerous to other goats. If it is CL, the pus from the abscess will be greenish and odorless and may be lumpy rather than smooth. Humans may also be able to contract this disease if they come into contact with this pus, although it is extremely rare. However, I would still take precautions when handling a goat with CL, especially if you have any cuts or open wounds. Wear gloves and always wash your hands after contact.

Treatment

If you believe one of your goats has CL, you should isolate them immediately and contact your vet, who will take a sample of the pus and send it off for testing. They will also be able to provide up to date information on how to proceed should your goat test positive for CL. Assuming you take them before any abscesses burst then usually they will recommend that the abscess is properly lanced and cleaned – ideally by the vet rather than the owner - and the goat is then kept away from other goats for at least thirty days until the abscess is completely healed up, as this way the infection cannot spread.

I will point out here that not all abscesses mean CL, so you should go to the vet as soon as you spot any. If the vet says it isn't CL, then you can use hot compresses and wait for them to rupture naturally rather than having the vet lance them. This will usually take up to a week and the abscess, once burst, should heal. The pus from a non-CL abscess is usually white and smooth.

If you did have a lactating doe tested positive for CL, the milk should be pasteurized before being used regardless of whether it is being consumed by goat kids or humans. If the abscess was on the udder then the milk should be thrown immediately. Any kids that were feeding from the affected doe should be removed from her and bottle raised. I would also get them tested just to be certain it hasn't been passed on.

Prevention
Again this is another disease that shouldn't affect you as a pet owner as long as you ensure that the goats you purchase have been tested before you buy them. This is also another reason to visit a herd in person rather than buying without seeing because you will be able to check all the animals for abscesses so you can be confident that none of the goats the seller owns have this disease.

There are two CL vaccines available in some countries but there are side effects associated with each. It is also worth noting that once the vaccine has been given, any subsequent tests will always be positive because the vaccine contains the bacteria that causes CL. Therefore, when purchasing you should ask the seller if they have vaccinated against CL because this could be a reason for some or all of their animals testing positive. In my opinion, if you are just owning a couple of goats as pets then you don't need to vaccinate because if your goat doesn't have it when they arrive on your property then they should never contract it unless you introduce new goats to them. Again, if you were ever replacing a goat you would need to have the test done before bringing the new ones onto your property. The vaccination is more appropriate for large herds especially those that are being raised for breeding and milking purposes.

Johnes (Pronounced Yo-Knees) Disease

Johnes Disease is caused by bacteria called Mycobacterium Avium Subspecies Paratuberculosis (MAP). It is a fatal gastrointestinal disease that is found in goats and other ruminants such as cattle, sheep, deer and so on.

The infection is contagious and is usually spread via the manure of the infected animal. MAP bacteria develops in the small intestine and is passed out via feces. If these are swallowed with feed, grass, water or milk for instance, the healthy goat will be infected. If a doe is infected, the disease can be present in her colostrum and milk, which is why kids are very susceptible and unlike with CAE, heat treatment on the milk isn't sufficient enough to kill the MAP organisms.

Usually, once an owner discovers that one of their goats has Johnes Disease, the rest of the herd have already become infected. Therefore, if you suspect Johnes Disease in one goat you should isolate it and get every goat you own tested too as well as any other ruminant animals you may have.

Unfortunately, once the signs appear, the goat will most likely already be at the end of life stage.

There is no vaccine yet that has been approved and sadly there is no cure. The best you can do is try to prevent Johnes Disease from being brought onto your property.

Symptoms
A goat can appear entirely healthy yet be infected with Johnes Disease and symptoms may not appear for a few months or even years later. This is why it's very important to ensure that the goats you buy have been tested and are free from the disease, as are the others in the herd it was born into. Usually a goat will become infected within their first few months of life.

Symptoms can be vague and are similar to many other illnesses and include diarrhea and rapid weight loss despite eating well. Eventually, the goat will become thin and weak. In order to get a diagnosis you will need a lab test from a vet.

Prevention

As I mentioned, there is no cure, so therefore the best you can do is prevent it. The good news is if you are just buying a couple of goats as pets it is another case of as long as the goats have been tested beforehand and you are buying them from a Johnes Disease free herd there is no reason for you to ever worry about this disease.

Again, if you introduce new goats or new ruminants onto your property you will need to get these tested as well before bringing them onto your land, otherwise there is a risk of bringing the disease with them.

As tempting as it may be, don't ever let anybody bring goats or ruminants onto your land without making sure they have been tested and clear of Johnes Disease and don't take your goats to anyone else's property either unless you are sure that it is safe to do so.

You will most likely be feeding your goats whatever they can forage on your property as well as the goat feed and hay you bring in, but if you do bring forage from other areas outside of your property then make sure it hasn't come from a place where other ruminants may have previously grazed just in case those animals had the disease. This is more a precaution, however than a serious concern because at the time of writing, free ranging ruminants such as deer or elk are thought to be free of the MAP infection and it is more apparent in those animals in captivity.

Practice good hygiene by keeping your goat areas as free of manure as possible and change bedding, water and feed regularly, especially if you notice feces in it. Again, if you raise the feed equipment there shouldn't be a risk of this happening.

If you do have goats that are being milked or that have babies that they are feeding then try to clean the does udders wherever possible before the kids nurse and before milking as suckling or milking from manure stained teats can increase the risk of spreading the infection.

If you do have goats that are diagnosed with Johnes Disease, don't immediately go out and buy more pet goats after they have passed on. The MAP organism is very hardy (they're rather like the cockroaches of the organism world) and can survive in the environment. It is resistant to damp, drying, heat and cold and whilst the majority will die out after several months without animals being present, a few can remain for up to eleven months in soil and seventeen months in water albeit in low levels. Therefore, before purchasing more goats you would need to thoroughly wash and disinfect every part of your garden, goat shed, feeding equipment and water troughs several times and leave to dry out to ensure all the bacteria has definitely been eradicated. Just remember, if you wash out a water trough and feeding equipment, don't dump the slimy dirty water onto the ground, as if there are organisms in there it will just infect the soil! I would recommend thoroughly disinfecting and leaving the area animal free for at least a year before bringing in any more pets just to be on the safe side.

Bloat
This is when air bubbles form in the rumen and get trapped. It is usually caused by high quantities of unsuitable food, for instance eating too much grain or wet grass pastures, which can cause frothy bloat.

Symptoms
Bloat is incredibly uncomfortable for a goat and you may notice them kicking their left side and grunting. Their left side may also be hard and swollen. Sometimes a goat will lie on their left side, but this makes the condition worse because it traps the gas even more.

You may think that bloat sounds a lot like trapped wind in a human but it is a far more serious condition and can result in death if left untreated.

Treatment
To relieve the symptoms of bloat, the air bubbles in the goat's rumen need to be broken down. You can help by massaging the goat's flank then trying to get them to walk about. If possible, elevate your goat on an incline so that their front legs are higher than their rear as this can help the gas escape.

Another option is to mix Baking Soda into your goat's feed, as this can also take away bloat.

Some people recommend giving a vegetable oil and dish soap mixture if your goat is suffering from frothy bloat, however other people disagree and believe that the vegetable oil will add to a goat's discomfort. If you believe that your goat has frothy bloat, mineral oil or milk of magnesia may be a better choice in breaking down the tiny bubbles in their rumen.

If none of these solutions work, you should contact a vet. They may prescribe a course of Penicillin or they may pass a tube into the goat's stomach in order to release the pressure in the rumen.

Prevention
Some goats may look bloated when in fact they simply have a full stomach, but they should be able to pass wind or bring up cud easily. A goat with bloat will be in obvious discomfort and will appear distressed so if they look bloated but are happily chewing or playing then you shouldn't need to panic.

Bloat can usually be prevented by feeding a balanced diet, rationing their food and introducing new feeds gradually.

Urinary Calculi
This is a condition that affects male goats and is similar to Kidney Stones in a human. Crystals form in the urinary tract and block the flow of urine.

If the blockage isn't removed, the urine has nowhere to go and eventually causes the bladder to rupture, which will lead to death. It is a very painful condition and is one of the leading causes of death in male goats.

Symptoms
You may notice your goat is stretching and straining to urinate, yet they either don't produce anything at all or only manage a few small dribbles. You may notice that any urine they do produce is dark in

color or contains blood. The goat may also act constipated or you may notice a swelling or discoloration of their penis.

Your goat may stand hunched over or may continually press their head against the fence or walls. They may moan or cry or look like they are in distress, especially when they are trying to urinate.

Other symptoms include shaking their head, a dull looking coat, white gums, shivering, worn out or hanging tail and teeth grinding.

Treatment
Unfortunately, treatment can be very challenging and isn't always successful unless it is caught early and treated immediately.

If your goat is straining but able to pass some urine, then a drenching with an Ammonium Chloride solution can be enough to break up the tiny crystals.

There are other 'at home' remedies but because your goat can become ill very quickly I would always recommend that you treat these animals like you would any other pet and consult a vet before trying to cure your goat yourself.

Usually a surgical procedure is needed to release the blockage. The best-case scenario is that the stones have collected in the end of the penis and can be snipped off. However, if the blockage is very severe and further up in the urinary tract then the surgical options can be very expensive and aren't always guaranteed to work. Even if the goat is cured the goat will have a higher chance of developing Urinary Calculi in the future.

If you believe your goat has Urinary Calculi then DO NOT force them to drink water. You cannot simply 'flush' it out and the more water they drink the quicker their bladder will fill up and eventually it will burst.

Prevention
Urinary Calculi is often caused by improper feeding. A Calcium to Phosphorous Ratio of 2:1 in their food is important so you need to

check everything you give them if you are buying store bought food and try to avoid too much grain.

Wethers are also prone to Urinary Calculi because castration stops testosterone being produced and this is the hormone that is responsible for the Urethra growing. If the males are castrated too early before their Urethra has time to grow then this can put them at risk of developing this condition. As a pet owner you probably won't be banding or getting your goat castrated unless you have bought a buck and then changed your mind, but you should check if you are buying a wether that they haven't been banded or castrated before 12 weeks of age.

Foot Scald and Foot Rot
Goats have a cloven hoof, which means that their hooves are split in the center. This space can trap manure, dirt and moisture, where bacteria and fungus thrive. If a hoof becomes overgrown, the outer edges start to fold underneath and this can also then trap bacteria, which lead to foot problems.

Symptoms
Foot Scald is the precursor to Foot Rot, so the symptoms are very similar. Usually you will notice your goat lifting their leg up or limping because it is a painful condition. They may even stay on their front knees to avoid putting any pressure on the hoof or hooves that are affected.

You may also notice a distinct and unpleasant odor coming from the foot.

Treatment
This includes soaking your goats' hooves in copper sulfate or zinc sulfate. You can also buy over the counter products if you have caught it early enough. Before treating you will need to trim the hoof first.

Prevention
Warm, wet weather conditions can make Foot Scald and Foot Rot develop quicker. The best way to prevent this condition is to keep

your goats' feet trimmed regularly to avoid giving the bacteria and fungus a place to develop.

Coccidiosis
Coccidia are parasites that live and grow within the cells that line the gastro-intestinal tract. It is another disease that is transmitted if a goat eats feces that are infected with the eggs of these parasites.

Symptoms
Symptoms will usually appear around five to thirteen days after contracting this disease. The main ones are loss of appetite, dehydration and weakness. You may notice that your goat has diarrhea that may be bloody and dark but sometimes you may notice normal looking stools that smell foul. If this is left untreated the goat will eventually die.

Treatment
If you believe that your goat has Coccidiosis then you need to treat it immediately. Send a stool sample to your vet and ask for treatment. Usually drugs such as Baycox are prescribed.

Prevention
These parasites are always present in the environment, so all goats will be infected with a small number, but they do very little damage unless it gets out of control. Adult goats usually have robust immune systems and so can resist an outbreak of Coccidia but young or sick goats can be affected as can those that are older or stressed.

The best way to prevent is to keep your goat enclosure and barn as clean as possible, feed off the ground to prevent them accidentally eating feces with their food, making sure your feeders and water troughs are cleaned regularly and any feces are removed promptly and keeping your goats as happy and stress free as possible. If you believe any of your goats are infected then separate from the rest until they have been completely treated, especially if there are any baby kids or older goats on the property.

Common Goat Behavior

Goats are energetic and playful yet can be happy spending a lot of time in one spot, so if you see them sat for long periods it doesn't necessarily mean that they are sick and this on its own shouldn't be a cause for concern.

Your goats should enjoy playing together and being in each other's company but a sick goat will often isolate itself so you should keep an eye on them and make sure they play together at least some of the time.

Anglo Nubian Goats have a reputation for being noisy and whilst some can be, they only tend to make noise when they need something. If you have at least two goats and know that you are feeding them properly, are giving them fresh water regularly and have provided the perfect living environment then they may be crying because they are ill. If you listen carefully to your goat, eventually you should be able to distinguish between a normal 'happy' bleat and one that is distressed. For example, your goat may bleat when it is hungry or you may notice your goat bleating in hot weather because it is thirsty. Usually these bleats start off quiet and become louder over time.

A healthy bleat may sound 'livelier' whereas a goat that is in pain will have a different tone; much like a human who is in pain will have a different cry to one who isn't.

Talk to the breeder when you purchase your goat, as they may be able to provide information on the goat's behavior and noises.

Signs Of A Sick Goat

Other than a different tone when bleating and isolating themselves from their friends there are other general signs you can look out for:

- Teeth Grinding
- Diarrhea or feces that aren't 'normal'
- Difficulty urinating or showing pain when trying to urinate
- Bloated or hard stomach
- Lack of interest in drinking or refusing to drink

- Lack of interest in food or refusing to eat
- High temperature – anything above 38.6 degrees Celsius/101.5 degrees Fahrenheit is classed as a subnormal temperature. A temperature of 39.7 degrees Celsius/103.5 degrees Fahrenheit or above is a fever
- Pressing their head against fences or walls
- Kicking or biting their stomach
- Head shaking
- Green or cloudy nasal discharge
- Rapid breathing or abnormally slow breathing
- Pale or grey eyelids
- Standing hunched over
- Lying on their side or not moving for hours on end
- Weight loss without a loss in appetite.

Should I Call A Vet?

If you are a farmer and are experienced with animals then there may be some things you can do yourself at home, however as a pet owner you should treat these animals as you would a dog or a cat, so my advice would always be that if you suspect your goat is ill then consult a vet, especially if your goat is isolating itself, lying down in one spot for hours on end, appears lifeless or is moaning in pain.

Vet bills can be expensive, especially as you will need one who specializes in livestock, so it may be wise to see if it is possible to get your goat insured or to put away money in a savings account, as this way you will be paying out small amounts each month rather than having to fork out a large lump sum if your goat does get sick for any reason.

Chapter 8: Goat Shows

Why Show A Goat?
As a pet owner, taking your animal to a show can be great fun, kind of like beauty pageants for goats.

Attending these shows is a good way for you to share your hobby with others who have a love of goats, because you will meet many breeders and owners that you can talk to and share anecdotes and care tips and if you are in any doubt about how to care for your beloved pet you can ask questions - most people will love the chance to share their knowledge.

Some judges will talk to you individually after a show, so you can get advice on why your goat didn't place (if this is the case) or how you can improve next time.

As well as learning about what makes a 'good' Anglo Nubian Goat, shows are also beneficial because they often gain publicity, which encourages breeders to continually breed only the best animals and strive to continually improve bloodlines. Anyone who breeds and enters animals into shows can gain recognition this way, which makes it easier to sell their goats in the future, so if you were going to breed, whether it be to make money or just so you are provided with a natural source of milk, then it may be worth considering attending goat shows as a way of advertising your animals and building up a reputation in the goat world.

If you don't want to breed you can still make connections with those that do; should you ever want a new goat either to make your herd bigger or to replace one that dies then by attending shows you will be better placed at finding a breeder with excellent animals.

Before Showing
There are often forms to fill out in order to register your goat for a show. Find all the shows in your area that you would like to attend for that year, list them in date order and request all the paperwork early so you are able to get it sent back before the deadline.

Read everything carefully so you understand exactly what classes are available and are suitable for you and your goat. Check that the goat(s) you want to show don't have any faults that will disqualify them such as faults with their teats or mouth defects. Those that don't qualify or that aren't registered can be entered into pet classes. These are more informal (usually children enter) but the goats will still be judged on confirmation, condition, presentation and temperament and rosettes will be awarded to the winners.

Approved shows will only accept goats that are registered and in most countries you will need to be part of a goat club in order to take part. These groups will have their own set of guidelines and rules to follow as well as those of the show so make sure you are up to date with all of these before you attend, otherwise you could be disqualified.

Some shows may run over two days, so these may not be appropriate if you are travelling a long way, as you would have to find somewhere for both you and your goat to stay overnight.

The Show Ring

Whilst I can describe a show ring and what is expected of you, watching somebody else do it may be more beneficial, so you should attend at least one or two shows before you take part. If you don't want to do this then you may find some of the videos that have been posted online helpful to watch so you don't feel embarrassed on the day if you're not sure what you are doing.

A show line will often lead off from the left and you will be expected to walk around the ring in a clockwise direction, but it is entirely up to the judge on the day so this can vary.

Make sure there is enough room between your goat and the goat in front; the last thing you want is to get disqualified because your goat has nipped another goat's rump!

What About Me?

Technically, the judge should be judging your goat and not you. However, you should try to be as professional as possible as this will always go in your favor. The judge will warm to you more if you are taking the show seriously rather than larking about in the show ring.

Some shows will allow you to wear what you like whilst others will require 'show whites', which means a clean white top and clean white trousers, or in some countries it is a white coat, so as not to detract from the goats. Some open shows or those that are part of a larger agricultural show may be flexible about their dress code, but you should always check if this is required when you sign up for the show.

If you are taking part in a US 4H show then please note that these are very strict about proper show attire.

Attitude

Don't go into a show expecting to win; without wanting to sound condescending it is highly unlikely that you will win the grand prize on your first show, however this doesn't mean you have to go in with a defeatist attitude either.

Both you and your goat will be nervous, which is entirely normal, so take part with the attitude that you are both there to gain experience and to have fun, that way if you don't win anything you won't be too disappointed.

If you don't place as high as you'd hoped (or if you don't place at all) don't feel upset, take on board the judge's comments and if possible talk to them after the show to find out how you can improve for future competitions.

If you're not sure what you are doing pretend that you do and copy the person in front. Try to act confident even if you don't necessarily feel it; stand tall, hold your head up high and smile. Not only will you impress the judges but it may help your goat to relax and be confident too.

Illnesses

Most shows should ask for proof that the goats have been CAE, CL and Johnes Disease tested, but there are plenty of other illnesses that goats may have and whilst it shouldn't happen let's be realistic; people will show sick goats. You may not be able to tell that they are ill by looking at them and their owners may not even be aware of it, but think very carefully before showing your pet, as there is always a chance they could catch a serious disease.

There are precautions that can be taken, such as having a portable pen that you only use for shows or putting disposable tarpaulin or plastic sheets on the ground before placing bedding on them. You can even put tarpaulin between the pens so that your goat doesn't have direct contact with other goats whilst they are waiting to take part. However, they are going to have to mix with other goats in the ring, so there is no way you can make sure they are one hundred percent safe; it is more about limiting the amount of exposure they have with others.

If you are worried you can send your goat(s) to be tested after a show to ensure they haven't picked up any infection.

Preparation
Grooming
You don't necessarily have to bath, clip and brush your goat for a show, but it may reduce your chances of winning if you don't. Although judges do award points for conformation, if your goat shows up muddy with unkempt hair and overgrown hooves whilst others are immaculately groomed, the judge will most likely look more favorably on them. If nothing else you want your goat to look well cared for.

Grooming a goat may be a challenge if you haven't done it before, but the more you practice the easier it becomes. There are lots of videos online that you can watch to see how it's done. I would advise you clip two to three weeks prior to a show, as this will give you a chance to tidy up any areas you may have missed and also allows any bad lines to grow out.

Hooves should always be trimmed and cleaned two days before a show.

Many owners will bathe their goat before taking them to a show, which is fine, but be sure to use a suitable, good quality animal shampoo and rinse thoroughly to get all the soap out otherwise it could irritate your goat's skin and can make the coat dull rather than shiny.

Goats with horns usually aren't allowed to be shown, but if you have one that has scurs or buds, rubbing on a little Vaseline or hoof oil can shine these. The same goes for the hooves.

Handling
You will need to walk your goat around the showing arena, so you will need to get them used to this beforehand. A goat that is only handled for shows may struggle or freeze once they are in the show ring, because they are not used to it. To a judge (and other owners) this can look like you don't have control of your goat.

The best way to do this is to make it a part of their everyday life by walking them around your garden as much as possible using a show collar just like you would in a show. Just a short walk in a circle around their pen or barn is a good way to get them to feel comfortable. Remember the new surroundings of a show will be stressful enough for your goat, so the more you can get them used to what is expected of them beforehand the better.

Standing
As well as walking your goat, you will also be expected to correctly position them whenever the judge asks you to so that they can check their conformation and compare them to others taking part. Again, this should be practiced beforehand not only so that your goat can get used to you touching their legs and standing them in a certain way, but also to give you the confidence to quickly and easily adjust them whenever necessary.

When positioned, their back should be nice and straight with their back legs under their hips and their front legs under their shoulders. Their neck should be extended and their head should remain steady.

To get your goat used to the judges, let someone you know handle your goat and run their hands along their back so that they can get used to other people touching them as well as you. This should make them less skittish when they attend shows.

Another thing to practice is opening your goat's mouth whilst holding their lead because you will need to do this so that they judge can inspect their bite.

Talking quietly to your goat throughout their training and then during the shows can reassure and help calm them quicker if they are a little bit nervous in the ring.

What Should I Take?
The main things you will need at a show are a show collar and lead, a water bucket, feed and a bowl to put it in, hay – a hook on hay rack is also a good idea so that they don't have to eat directly from the ground – and a brush or comb so that you can groom your goat before they are called.

Most shows will provide bedding but I would always check this beforehand just to make sure, as you want your goat to be comfortable the whole time they are there.

You should also take a safety pin or a clip, as you may be given a goat number to pin on yourself.

Moving
In the UK, DEFRA movement regulations means that you are not allowed to move a goat unless you have an Animal Movement License. This means that if you want to take your goat to a show you will need one of these licenses for both the journey there and the journey back. Other countries will also require something similar because these animals are classed as livestock, so make sure you fill these out in advance because the Show Secretary will usually ask to see it on the day.

These can usually be done online but if you prefer you may also be able to obtain a paper copy.

On The Day

Upon arrival, you should find the Show Secretary and hand in all your paperwork. They will check everything is in order, complete any sections that apply to them and then hand you back the relevant documents that you need. They should then hand you a show number to wear on your clothes and direct you to your pen.

Settle your goat in their pen with food and water. Usually there should be some show organizers milling about who will be happy to show you where you can fill up your water bucket. Whilst you wait for your class to be called, you should have time for any last minute grooming.

Listen carefully for your class to be called. The steward or judge should show you where to stand and how to line up - usually it will be in numerical order.

How a show is organized is at the judge's discretion on the day, so each one may be different, but they usually follow the same pattern.

To start with, you will be asked to either line up in order to walk your goat around the ring in a circle so the judge can see how they walk on a lead, or you will be asked to stand in a line with the goat's rumps facing the judge so they can do their inspection first. Listen carefully to all instructions and copy what everyone else is doing.

The judge will examine each goat individually. This inspection will consist of seeing the 'bite', looking at the feet and checking for any teat faults. During this time, you will be expected to keep your goat as still as possible.

The judge may then ask you to walk your goat in a straight line. Often this is done in pairs so that they can compare your goat to another. Once you have done this, you may be asked to stand your goat facing either to the right or to the left so that they can look at their profile.

Once everyone has been examined you will be asked to walk in a circle so that the judge can see how each goat moves.

Whenever your goat is stood in a line up you should ensure that they are positioned correctly with their legs apart, back straight and head held high, as this will help the judge to see their conformation and make their decision.

At the end you may be asked to move into a line according to placement. Don't get too elated or upset early on, as you may be asked to move again if the judge changes their mind, so listen carefully for your number just in case you are asked to swap places.

Once the judge is satisfied with their decision the rosettes will be given out and the judge will explain the reasons why each goat placed as they did. If you aren't as high as you wanted or you don't place you can learn what to improve on in the future.

First place winners from each class will compete at the end for 'best in show' or 'grand champion'.

Tips
- Always check the rules and regulations for your show before you attend – there's nothing worse than travelling miles for a show only to find you are disqualified because your animal doesn't meet the right criteria.
- Practice walking and standing before a show, because even the most well behaved goat may end up having 'stage fright' on the day. Remember they are in a completely different environment to what they are used to at home. Practicing before a show gets them used to what is required of them so this at least can be familiar and not as frightening.
- Trim their hooves so that the judge can see that your goat can walk correctly and doesn't have any defects. Always comb and clip your goat according to goat standards.
- Dress appropriately yourself. If you are required to wear certain clothes then do. Whilst you shouldn't be disqualified for wearing the wrong attire, it certainly won't help you make a good impression.
- Always keep your goat between you and the judge; if the judge is at the goat's rear you should stand at the front. As

the judge moves around to the right and towards the goat's front you should step round to stand on the left hand side of the goat. This prevents you from getting in the judge's way or blocking their view.

- Keep an eye on the judge at all times, as they will tell you what they would like you to do. They may also ask you questions, which you may miss if you aren't paying attention.
- Don't ever talk to the person next to you. This is considered very rude and can distract the judge. The whole time you are in the ring you should be focused on the judge and your goat.
- Always remain calm. Your goat - whilst a pet and possibly in your eyes a member of your family - is also an animal and they won't always behave the way you want them to. This can be frustrating, but try not to get worked up and lose your temper. Never shout, hit or treat your goat roughly. Remember your goat may be scared, bored or just in a mood and getting worked up won't help. Show that you aren't fazed by their bad behavior by remaining calm. This will make you seem professional and will go in your favor.
- Always be a good winner or a good loser. There's nothing worse than someone who sulks or storms off just because their goat hasn't placed. However disappointed you may feel on the inside, don't let it show. Take time to congratulate the winners and those who placed ahead of you. Take all comments on board so that you can improve for future shows.

Chapter 9: Horns

There are many controversial topics when it comes to goats and as silly as it sounds, horns are at the top of the list, with each owner having their own opinion.

Some will say that the horns are natural and should be kept intact whilst others will say they are the mark of the devil and should be removed as soon as possible!

Should I Keep My Goats' Horns?

A common argument for keeping horns is that they protect goats from predators and are their only defense mechanism. To me this is a myth. Firstly, goats are prey animals in the wild, which means that many creatures will hunt them for food. Goats have a 'flight or fight' instinct and most of the time they would prefer to run rather than fight. If cornered then yes they would use their horns to defend themselves but, as sad as it is, the majority of the time this won't save them, not in the wild and not in your back garden.

As an owner you are the one who is responsible for your goats being safe from predators and this is done with a secure fence and shed, not horns, so if your reason for keeping your goat's horns is to keep them safe then get rid of them. Trust me, horns will most likely do your goat (and the rest of the household) more harm than good.

I will point out here that I do think horns look great, but I don't believe that just because they may be more aesthetically pleasing they should be left on a domesticated goat. I also happen to think that Anglo Nubian Goats look just as cute without the horns! My opinion, based on my personal experiences and in depth research, is that goats in captivity should not be kept with their horns.

The reasons for this are as follows:

Firstly, although they may well be natural, horns can cause a goat a lot of problems. Yes, if they are wild goats living out in natural habitat they are not going to encounter fences and other obstacles, but as a pet they are going to have limited space and be fenced in every single day and, as I mentioned before, goats are inquisitive and they will most likely try to escape on a daily basis. Horns do not aid this. In fact, horns can be very detrimental even to a goat that isn't trying to escape. They can get caught on fences, feeders and a number of other things. A goat doesn't understand how to dip the end of their horns back down to pass back through the hole, therefore they end up getting stuck.

You may think this might be cute and if you're around twenty four seven and happen to catch them doing this then yes, I can see how a goat who has it's horn stuck in a fence can be cute, you snap a quick picture and set them free, what's the harm? However, if you happen to be at work or wherever and are not around, if the goat gets themselves stuck they can end up being seriously injured or even killed.

It is true that a goat who hasn't got horns can still get their head stuck, but horns are just an extra liability.

Aside from getting stuck, horns can get damaged and this can be very painful for a goat. Given the fact that you should always have a minimum of two goats, horns can easily be broken off through fighting or playing and if they are pulled off completely there can be an open wound that can bleed – a lot! This is because once they are fully-grown these horns will contain blood vessels.

As well as accidentally injuring each other, your goat(s) may use their horns as a weapon, which can not only damage their own horns but those of their playmates too. You will often see two goats head butting each other, but sometimes a goat will run into the other ones side rather than rushing it head on. They may then suddenly jerk their head backwards and up. This movement with horns can cause serious damage.

Thirdly, you should consider your own safety and that of others in your household or visitors. Whilst you shouldn't allow your goats to get into the habit of head butting you anyway, even when young, if they head butt you and they have horns it can be incredibly painful!

Remember that these animals are livestock and they don't have to be on the attack to cause damage. When feeding, watering, trimming hooves, petting, bathing, grooming, milking and all the other number of things you will do to care for your pet, you will be in close proximity to their heads. You could be bent down to give them a cuddle, they move their head the wrong way and you've lost an eye!

If you have children that live with you or just have friends and relatives that visit with kids, then horns are a definite NO! One wrong move by a child or a goat (and believe me, both are unpredictable!) and you have a badly injured child!

If you are milking your goats then you will need to use a milking stand and horns aren't accommodated for on these contraptions, which means you will need a set up that allows you to milk safely, whether this is buying a custom built stand or making one yourself – either way it could be more costly and inconvenient than simply getting rid of your goats' horns to begin with.

Most organisations and agricultural shows (including 4H in America) don't allow you to enter goats that have horns for the safety of both the goats and humans. Originally another reason for no horns is that it sets apart the 'show standard' goats from the 'common' goats that would be found out in the wild.

I think that you should also consider what the future will hold for your goat. In an ideal world, you will keep them for the whole of their lives, but if your circumstances change and you end up having to sell your goats then the chances of rehoming them are considerably lower if they have horns because – for all the reasons given above – most people do not want a goat that has intact horns.

A non-safety reason for keeping horns is that they are necessary to regulate your goat's body temperature, but I don't agree with this.

I'm not disputing the fact that horns are vascular, which means they can give out heat. Plenty of research has proven that goats in desert climates have longer horns with a thinner outer layer to allow for more heat to be released, whereas goats living in cooler climates have smaller, thicker horns to prevent too much heat being released.

What I do dispute is that goats need their horns to regulate their body temperature, because if this were true then in the summer all those goats that were naturally polled, disbudded or banded would be dying as soon as the hot weather hit. If horns were needed to regulate body heat then naturally polled goats wouldn't exist because the goats used to reproduce the gene that eliminates horns wouldn't have been able to mate and give birth if they were dying from heat exhaustion. Whilst I agree with the fact that horns can help with regulating the body temperature of a goat, I don't believe this their horns are the only way they do this.

The opposite must also be true too; in colder weather the heat must still be lost via the horns in winter and therefore it can make your goat colder in winter.

Another reason given for keeping horns is that getting rid of them is a non-medical and unnatural procedure. However, there are many things we do to our pet goats that are non-medical and aren't natural – castration for one, also tattooing and ear branding, injections to prevent certain illnesses and so on. All of these actions cause some level of pain and discomfort for a short period of time and removing horns is no different. The long-term benefits outweigh the short-term discomforts, and it is not a cruel or mean thing to do.

Options
So what options do you have for getting rid of horns? It is either disbudding, banding or having them surgically removed. I will go through each option individually.

Disbudding

The Procedure
This is the safest, fastest and most humane way to remove horns. Not only is it done when the goats are very young so they will quickly forget about it, but it is done before the horns even start to grow.

It is done with a very (very!) hot disbudding iron, which will burn off the horn bud, killing the tissue so that the horn cannot grow. This specially made iron sterilizes and cauterizes the area so that there is no bleeding and a minimal risk of infection. Whilst it is painful, the whole process from start to finish only lasts about twenty seconds. Once it's over with the goats are usually straight back to nursing or drinking a bottle and they soon forget it. Occasionally, mild localized swelling can occur but this is very rare.

Scabs usually fall off after approximately two to four weeks and the hair will grow back soon after.

I'm not going to go into the details of how to disbud because most responsible breeders would not sell a goat with horns as a pet for all the reasons listed above and so disbudding should ideally be done before you take your new goat home. The other reason for having the breeder do it is that the baby can then run straight back to its mom to nurse.

If you are breeding your own goats then feel for the goat buds when born and check every day. Male buds will grow faster than females because of their hormone levels, but it is usually around three to ten days when they appear.

If you did wish to learn how to do it then there are plenty of videos online, however I believe that if you are only keeping a couple of goats as pets as opposed to running a farm with dozens of them then you don't really need to know how to do it yourself because you should be able to pay somebody to do it for you. Not all vets will disbud, but if you can find another goat owner living nearby who is experienced they may charge you a nominal fee, around £10 in the UK or $5-$10 dollars in the USA depending on your location.
It needs to be done properly, otherwise it can cause problems for your goat in later life and if the iron is held on too long it can cause brain damage. If the iron isn't held on long enough then scurs can occur.

Scurs

These occur when the horn tissue isn't properly burned away, so the leftover tissue can continue to grow over time. They can come in all shapes and sizes and most of the time they just look unsightly, like deformed horns. You will need to keep an eye on them, as they can break easier than horns, which can cause blood loss, open wounds and lead to infection if left untreated.

Sometimes scurs can grow backwards and curl towards the head – if this happens they need to be removed by a vet.

Banding

For older goats that haven't been disbudded, horns can be banded with castration bands. You can purchase these online, although I would always recommend that as a pet owner that you consult a vet.

The Procedure

The band is placed at the base of the horn. For the first couple of hours it will annoy the goat, causing them to thrash about trying to knock it off. After a few hours the 'feeling' in the horn will be lost - kind of like if you tied an elastic band really tightly around your finger. At this point the goat will appear oblivious and as an owner you will think the worst is over. However, the band will then begin to cut off the blood supply and this is when it becomes VERY PAINFUL for the goat.

Eventually the goat will be in a lot of pain and will become too frightened to move because whenever they do the horn will wiggle. They will avoid their playmates and possibly even their humans and they will most likely stop eating. This is a risky stage because if the horn falls off before the blood supply is fully stopped and the horn is dead the goat will bleed a lot. If you are not around to help them then they could potentially die.

If all goes well however, there will be minimal blood loss. The whole process takes around four to six weeks from banding the horn to it falling off, plus another two to three week for it to completely heal.

Whilst it may sound like a relatively simple procedure, many owners will avoid banding horns. As well as it being painful, stressful and risky, your goat will become distrustful of you and won't want them near their head for a very, very long time. They may even avoid you altogether and if these goats are your pets it can be sad to find that they are no longer playful towards you. If you had a tame and friendly goat it may take you a long time to get them back to the sweet-natured, loving creature they were before the banding.

If your goats have horns that are causing damage, constantly getting caught on fences, being used to bully other goats or terrorize you and your family then banding is the best alternative, but if you buy your goats from birth then I would urge you to either buy ones that have been disbudded or to disbud them yourself.

Surgery
You can have a vet remove the horns from an older goat, but as well as the expense it is also a major surgical procedure. Goats don't do well under anesthetic, so they may not even survive the operation, but if they do it is not a nice operation.

The Procedure
The vet will put your goat to sleep and then cut out the horn buds. This procedure will leave an open wound, leading into the goat's nasal cavity. Afterwards, there will be lots of drainage and oozing from the site and you will need to change their bandages on a daily basis.

Remember that these animals are livestock and live outdoors and no matter how much you clean they are going to be urinating and defecating and an open wound will put them at a high risk of infection.

Again this is a risky, stressful and painful procedure and should only be done if it is your only option.

Can I Cut My Goat's Horns Or Scurs Off?
If you are wondering if you can just cut your goats horns off with a saw or other sharp instrument the answer is NO!

I believe many people think goats' horns are like human fingernails or hair, as in you don't really feel them and if someone cuts them you barely even notice. Goats horns however aren't like this at all, there are major arteries running through there. Even scurs will contain blood vessels, so rather than comparing it to someone trimming your nails you should compare it to someone chopping off your arm…without anesthetic!

Cutting a goat's horns off is painful and inhumane and I do not recommend it at all. The goat will start to bleed heavily and if this isn't stopped immediately they will bleed to death in a matter of minutes. Stopping a goat from bleeding will not be as easy as you think either because they will be thrashing around and you will need to put a huge amount of pressure on.

So no, chopping off your goats' horns yourself is not an option!

Polled

A goat that is born hornless is known as polled. You will be able to feel two rounded bumps on their head but their horns will never grow.

Breeders can ensure that goats don't have horns by breeding those with the polled gene. An easy way to explain it is to say that goat DNA has two slots for the horn gene. One slot gets filled by the mother and one by the father. If two goats are bred and they both have the horn gene then the babies that are born will have horns. Likewise if both parents have the polled gene then the kids will have no horns. If however one parent has the horned gene and one parent has the polled gene, then any kids that they have will be given both the horn gene and the polled gene. The horned gene is recessive and the polled gene is dominant, so in this case the babies will be born polled.

Being born polled means that they don't need to be disbudded and as nobody really likes the disbudding process one wonders why more breeders don't breed polled goats. I believe the reason is that a report was published stating that breeding polled goats increases the risk of the babies being hermaphrodites, meaning that the kids would be born with both male and female reproductive organs and therefore be sterile so would be unable to breed. Due to this report many breeders stopped breeding polled goats whilst others stopped registering their polled goats or tried to disguise them as being disbudded.

Whilst breeding specific traits in any animals comes with health risks, it is worth noting that not enough research has been done into this when it comes to breeding goats to be polled and I don't believe there is enough evidence to say whether it should be done or not.

Some breeders believe that it is fine as long as two polled goats aren't bred together, whilst others have bred polled to polled and say that there is no more risk of producing sterile animals as there is when breeding any two animals.

If you don't want to disbud or band but you don't want horns then it may be worth looking for a breeder that offers polled Anglo Nubian Goats. As long as you do the usual health checks as you would with any other animal then you shouldn't have any problems.

Conclusion
Whether you keep your goats' horns or not is entirely up to you. The aim of this chapter is to provide you with the necessary information so you can make an informed decision.

I would consider whether you really want to be ducking and diving to avoid horns or do you want a pet that you can cuddle? All too often pet goats end up being rehomed, locked up or tied to fence posts because their owner has realized that their cuddly pet is too dangerous even when they're being friendly.

Whilst I personally wouldn't keep a goat with horns as a pet I do understand why many want to. Just remember though that if you decided to get rid of your goats' horns in the future it can be more painful, stressful and dangerous the older the animal is. I believe it is much kinder to disbud a goat at a young age then put them through the stress of banding or surgery.

Chapter 10: Breeding

Although you most likely won't want to breed, some pet owners do eventually decide to breed their animals and therefore this chapter has been included just in case.

Why Breed?

Some pet owners will decide that they want to milk their goats and of course the only reason female goats produce milk is to feed their young, therefore they need to be pregnant or have recently given birth in order for their milk to come in. This is a big reason why people who buy Anglo Nubian Goats as pets decide to breed, as goats' milk is delicious and many of those who are lactose intolerant or allergic to cows' milk find that they can actually drink goats' milk without any issues.

Another reason for breeding is because your pets are also your hobby and breeding them is one more facet to this. It gives you hands-on experience with caring a goat through pregnancy then rearing the babies from birth and can be incredibly exciting for somebody who truly loves these animals.

Many people will breed their goats because they wish to make money from selling the babies, however this isn't the money spinner a lot of people believe it is. Some people do make money from selling their babies and also make a bit of extra on the side by selling their goats' milk or products such as goats' milk soap. However, if you are selling products to members of the public you will most likely need a license to do so and at the time of writing many owners are reporting that their goats are not selling and they are having to lower the price. Therefore, I would think very carefully about breeding just to make extra money.

Whatever your reason is for breeding, I urge you to consider the practicalities of breeding. It is not cheap, as you will have to buy extra food, adjust your doe's diet plus feed and care for the babies when they arrive.

Not only will your food bills increase, but have you got the space to keep your original goats plus the babies? Sometimes one pregnancy can result in three to four kids or more. Even if you are planning on selling the babies you won't be able to do this immediately, as you need to wean them first and make sure they are all healthy, plus it will take time for you to find good homes for them to go to. Please be a responsible breeder and consider not only your reasons for breeding but also what will happen afterwards and put a plan in place before you put your doe with a buck.

Should I Breed Unregistered Goats?

So you have enough space and can afford to keep the babies until they are old enough to go to new homes. The next thing you need to consider is whether you are breeding registered, award winning show goats or fabulous milking stock?

If the goat you are planning to breed isn't registered then I would be tempted not to breed. To me it's kind of like breeding a mongrel or a pedigree dog; if you are going to breed only breed the best.

Ideally when breeding you should be aiming to strengthen and improve the bloodline; I mentioned above that selling baby goats can be difficult, but it is far easier if the goats are registered and you can have the added selling point of them being show goats or high quality milking stock or just amazing pets.

At What Age Can Goats Breed?

Anglo Nubian Goats can breed at a young age but that doesn't mean they *should,* it just means that they can. This means if you do have a male and female goat you should separate them by around four months.

Ideally, a male should be at least a year to before you breed them for the first time and a female should be at least 12-18 months or until they are half their adult minimum weight so for Anglo Nubian Goats this would be 67.6lbs or more. This is to ensure the goats are fully grown, strong and healthy enough for this task.

It is especially important for the female as often a freshner (that is a doeling that hasn't been bred before) can often have a single kid birth as opposed to a multiple kid birth. The risk is that single kids tend to be bigger because they have more space in the uterus to grow and this mean a more difficult birth for the mother.

To get the healthiest kids you should only breed the healthiest animals. Make sure the goats are a good weight, free from parasites and have had their vaccinations.

Buck Service

Right, you have a plan in place for after breeding and a registered doe suitable for the task. What you might not have is a buck, but before you rush out to buy one you should look into buck service, which is where you hire a buck from someone else.

Choose your buck very carefully. You want the babies to have all the strengths of your doe but none of her weaknesses, therefore think about what you like most about your doe and what characteristics you would like to change, then find a buck which has all of these qualities. For example, if you know your doe has a low milk supply and you want to increase this in the kids, then choose a buck that is from strong milk goats and can correct this weakness in your own bloodline. If you want kids that have perfect show confirmation then look for a buck with this. Most owners who hire their bucks out will know about their bucks' strengths and weaknesses and if you approach them with your list they should be able to find one that is suitable for you.

Generally, most buck owners will only breed to registered does, which is another reason to only breed a registered goat. Generally, the bucks' owner will ask to see your goats' papers before they loan you the buck. They will most likely want to do a health inspection to ensure your doe is healthy and free from disease, so don't be offended. In fact, you should do the same with their buck. The bucks' owner may also want to know the does' history such as where does she comes from, how long you have owned her and so on.

The rest is entirely down to you and the bucks' owner. Some owners may allow their buck to come to your property for breeding; others will prefer you to take your doe to them. There are pros and cons to each. For instance, if the buck is coming to you, then this may be easier from your point of view because the owners should bring and collect them, however the downside of this is you then have to look after a buck for a couple days and all this entails such as the noise and the smell. Unless of course they bring their stud and just wait a few hours – the problem with this is that the goats may not breed immediately.

If your doe is going to the buck then you will be taking and collecting them. Many buck services will work this way because they will often be providing this service for those who own dairy farms and bring in two or three does at a time. In this instance, you will need to be able to trust the owner enough to look after your doe, but most people who offer buck service are farm owners and professional breeders who know what they're doing, so I wouldn't worry too much as long as you have done your research on them and have got some references from other people who have used them if possible.

A buck service isn't usually that expensive. In the UK it costs around £50 and approximately £5 per day for boarding your doe. In the US, it is around $50 - $75 per doe. If you take your doe to the buck you usually get two visits included in this price. If you are boarding your doe then you may have to pay a few dollars boarding fee.

The Breeding Process
Once you know your doe is in heat and you have found a suitable buck then breeding is really just a matter of putting the two together.

Usually the buck will start pawing and stomping to show that he's interested. If the doe urinates, he may put his face in it. The pair may run around together for a while but then the doe will eventually start to wag her tail and stand still whilst she waits for the buck to mount her.

The problem with using a buck service is that some goats prefer to breed at night, which is why it is better if you can board your doe or keep the buck on your property for a few days.

92

How Do I Know If My Doe Is In Heat?

A goat's heat cycle is every 18-21 days, usually starting in August and depending on the doe it can last around 2-3 days.

Signs you can look out for include wagging her tail, mounting other does (assuming you have two or more) or letting the other does mount her, clear discharge, increased urination, fighting or being more aggressive towards you or the other goats she's housed with or bleating for no apparent reason. Anglo Nubian Goats can be incredibly loud when they're in heat and may scream or make moaning or blubbering sounds, similar to a buck in rut.

Sometimes does go into silent heat and don't show any symptoms, so if you are going to use a buck service and want to know if your doe is in heat you could use a buck rag, which is a cloth that has been rubbed over the male goat so that his scent is transferred onto it. If you wave this buck rag under your females nose and she shows interest then chances are she's in heat and it is a good time to put her with a male goat.

How Can I Tell If My Doe Is Pregnant?

The best way to tell if your doe is pregnant is the fact that she doesn't come into heat again so if you have monitored her and bred her when she showed signs of heat and three weeks later she doesn't have another heat cycle then chances are she's pregnant. You should still monitor her for a couple more cycles of twenty one days just to be sure she doesn't come into heat properly because some does can have 'false heat' which means they look like they are in heat and are put with a buck but actually they weren't and therefore three or four weeks later they start showing signs again. This happens most often with female goats that are being bred for the first time.

You may notice that your female has become more aggressive, whilst this could be a sign that she's in heat again it could also indicate pregnancy, especially if she starts challenging or fighting back against her herd mates.

Putting on weight is another symptom of pregnancy but this isn't always accurate in goats as they often look pregnant even when they're not but you may notice that your doe's abdomen is larger on the right side.

If you are already milking your goat then when she is pregnant her milk supply will start to reduce.

If your doe has never been bred before then around a month before her due date she should start to develop her udder – of course this is a late sign and you should really have identified that your female is pregnant before this stage.

The best way to find out if your female is pregnant is to allow the vet to do an ultrasound, which can be done thirty days after breeding, or a blood test which can be done sixty days after breeding.

Gestation Period

The gestation period – or length of pregnancy – for goats is around a hundred and fifty days, or approximately five months give or take, which is fairly short compared to some animals. Some does can take 155 days whereas some can deliver as early as 142 days. It is important to keep a close eye on your doe if she is pregnant and look for signs that she is about to give birth. It is especially important if she hasn't been bred before as she may need assistance.

An average litter will be two to three kids although it is not unusual for a goat that has been bred for the first time to have just one kid.

One Month Before Giving Birth

You should provide your female doe with a kidding stall in which to give birth with deep straw bedding.

A month before they're due to give birth make sure they receive a booster CD/T vaccination, as this will give them immunity, which they will pass on to their kids.

Increase their grain supply at this point because this final month is when the kids grow bigger and the doe will need extra nutrition, otherwise the kids will drain her body's reserves, which could make her weak and ill.

You should also trim your does' feet and clip her hair if the weather is warm in order for her to be comfortable when she gives birth. Once she's had the babies you will want to give her time to recover, so doing all this grooming beforehand means you won't have to do it so soon afterwards. If the weather is cooler just clip her udder, belly, back of the legs and under their tail area for hygiene reasons and to enable the goat to give birth and nurse without hair getting in the way.

Watch your doe very closely just in case you see signs that she is ready to give birth sooner than the hundred and fifty days' period.

Day Of The Birth

Ideally, as a pet owner, you should have a vet present when your goat gives birth unless you are an experienced breeder or an experienced goat farmer, so I'm not going to go into the details of how to assist with a birth. What you can assist with is providing clean towels and drying each one off after they are born. Clean their face and nostrils then place each baby in front of mom to clean and bond with. If there is more than one baby then keep the first ones in a towel and dry off whilst the doe continues to give birth. If you want your babies to 'land on' a clean towel then put one underneath your doe, as this can help keep clean up to a minimum.

Allow the kids to nurse and receive colostrum within twenty minutes of being born, as not only will this help settle them and allow them to bond with their mum, the colostrum will also provide antibodies to keep them healthy and help their immune systems.

After The Birth

Kidding can be stressful and leaves does more susceptible to parasites, so you should de-worm your doe the day after she gives birth. Make sure you check the label on the de-wormer to ensure it doesn't affect the milk and is safe for the kids to drink.

After four to five days you should give the newborn kids probiotics to help their rumens start working. This can be bought as a paste, which you can squeeze onto your finger and place on the roof of the kids' mouths.

After three to seven days your baby goats should be ready to disbud. You should start checking from day three, especially if you have bucks, as these tend to grow fairly quickly. Disbud them as soon as you can feel them if you are planning on getting rid of their horns.

Many breeders will give the kids a shot of Tetanus Toxoid to give them some immunity before their first shots at three weeks, however if you gave your doe a CD/T shot a month before her due date then the kids should have immunity anyway, so check with your vet whether this is necessary or not.

At one week old you can start to milk your doe for your own benefit even if the kids are nursing. If you do this at around one week then this will ensure that your goat starts to produce more milk overall. You should milk in the morning, then the kids can start to nurse throughout the day.

If you only have a single kid then check your female's udder because sometimes a lone kid can just feed from one side, which leaves the doe's udder uneven. If you milk the opposite side then you will actually be helping the doe out, because otherwise it can be painful if the milk isn't removed.

If your doe is a freshener – that is she's never been bred or milked before – then doing a small milking session will get her used to this. It's not a 'full' milking if the kids are nursing as well so she won't have to be as patient, but it will get her familiar to the routine and the milk stand and she will start to associate this with breakfast and treats, making it less stressful than if you just put her straight on the milk stand and take all her milk from her in one go.

At two weeks you should start to separate the kids from their mom at night. I would start this late in the beginning and give both the doe and the kids hay to nibble in order to distract them. Once they start to get used to it then you can separate a little bit earlier each night until eventually you are separating at dinner time.

It is important to consider whether you will be breeding before you build your barn so that you can have separate pens put in. Even though you are separating you can still keep your does and babies side by side with a fence between so they can still see and hear each other. I have seen barns that have separate pens but a shared metal hayrack so the goats are still eating together.

The reasons for separating are to get the goats used to being apart if you are selling but also so that the kids can nibble on their grain without their mother gobbling it all down.
Separating means you can go and play with the kids alone without their mother enabling you to bond without the doe interfering and allows you to bottle train them.

Another reason for separating is that you can milk the doe(s) in the morning without the kids running around or nursing before you get a chance to put your doe on the milking stand. Once you have milked you can put the goats all together again.

By three weeks the kids should all be eating well and you should be able to milk more for your own use. Kids should be vaccinated with a CD/T shot and also given Di-methox 12.5% (sulmet or corid) to prevent coccidiosis.

By seven weeks, your bucks and does should be separated full time. By this point you should put your bucks as far away from the females as possible to ensure that a baby doesn't impregnate other females in the herd including its sisters or mother. You should be aware that separating with a fence may not be enough because there have been stories of bucks impregnating females through fences and whilst these tend to be older goats I would still err on the side of caution and keep them fully apart.

Bottle Or Dam Raise?
Dam raising means allowing your kids to nurse from their mother until they are fully weaned, whereas bottle raising is just that – feeding your kids via a bottle of milk.

There are pros and cons to both. Dam raised kids tend to settle in the herd better and are more sociable with the other goats whereas bottle fed kids tend to be off by themselves more.

If you are keeping your kids then you may prefer them to be closer to their herd, but if you are planning on selling them then bottle raising may be best because it gets the kids used to people and stops them becoming too dependent on their mother.

Whichever you choose, handle each kid daily and spend time in the pens playing with them. Usually they will use you as a human climbing frame and will try to climb on your lap and over your back if you let them. This will enable them to be confident and sociable with humans, which is what you want if your goats are to become good pets either for you or for someone else.

Weaning

By eight to twelve weeks your kids will be ready to wean and they should be eating plenty of grain and hay and grazing. By this point they will be ready to be on their own full-time, which is when you can start to send them off to their new homes if you are selling them.

Before they leave you, it is sensible to have them fully weaned at least a week before they go to their new owners, as this is less stressful for them – although if they have been bottle fed from an early age it shouldn't make too much difference – and also means you can detect any problems should they arise before they are sold. The last thing you want is for a kid to be returned because their new owner is saying you've sold them a sick or unhealthy goat.

Milking

If you are breeding your pet goat so that you can have milk. then you should have lessons with an experienced owner who knows what they're doing in order to learn a good technique. If you know what you are doing you will get more milk out and in a shorter time it also improves your goat's mood, as they won't be stood around for too long and it will also help to keep your goat healthy. You should always maintain high standards of hygiene so that you don't put your goat at risk of mastitis or get poor tasting milk.

Once you are milking for your own consumption and the kids are weaned then you should milk twice a day to keep your goat comfortable.

To maintain this milk supply you will need to breed your female once a year. Your doe can get pregnant whilst she is lactating and you can continue to milk your goat whilst she is pregnant, however you should stop milking at least a couple of months before she is due to deliver and allow her milk supply to dry up so that her body has time to rest and build up a good nutritional reserve ready for the new babies she will have. There is nothing wrong with breeding purely for a milk supply, but please do so responsibly, your priority should be your doe's health.

A female Anglo Nubian Goat can live for around ten to fourteen years and once old enough to breed can continue to have babies for the whole of her life, although the older she gets the more complications can arise.

Points To Remember

Bucks will only breed when they smell a female that is in heat. Bucks go into rut, which is when they get a surge of hormones, and this can cause a doe to go into heat if they weren't previously. This is why males and females should be separated until you want them to breed. During rut males will spit, snort and urinate on themselves.

It is not unheard of for unwanted pregnancies to occur because males and females have been separated but kept in pens that are side by side – goats have been known to breed through fences so if you do want bucks and does on your property then they need to be kept well away from each other.

You should first take care of at least a couple of Anglo Nubian Goats for a few years and understand how to look after these creatures properly before you start to breed. Do plenty of research beforehand and make sure you have enough space as well as the time to look after them properly. I would also advise that you consult an experienced breeder and get their opinion and advice. Your animals' health should be your top priority. Remember there are hidden costs such as vet bills if one needs to be on hand for the birth, disbudding, vaccinations and castrating males as well as the extra food bills.

There can be complications with kidding – difficult births and abnormal presentation of the kids can occur, so make sure you have an experienced vet on hand to deliver as well as to guide you through the pregnancy.

If you use a buck service make sure both parties are clear on what this entails. How much will the service cost? Will the buck owner want one of the kids and will this be free or at cost price?

Make sure that you are selling to good owners who understand how to look after these animals. Remember that sudden dietary changes can make goats very ill, so make sure you give information on what you have been feeding them as well as other general information on how to look after them.

Breeding takes its toll on a doe's body, so whilst you will need to breed once a year to maintain milk supply, you shouldn't breed a single goat more than three times in two years. If you do want a constant supply it may be worth buying two or three does and taking it in turns in which one you breed to give the others chance to recover.

Chapter 11: Training

When you think of goats it may not even cross your mind that you can train them yet, like dogs, there are many different things they can learn to do.

Goats are smart and just repeating behavior over and over will help them to pick up certain actions. For example, if you stand in the same place every day and give your goat a treat, eventually you will find them standing in that spot waiting for you because they associate it with a treat.

It is easier to train younger goats but just as you can teach an old dog new tricks so can you teach an older goat, it just takes a bit more time and patience is all. The younger you can train your goats, the better, but more important than age is having a trusting relationship between you and your goats.

Bottle fed kids are easier to train than goats that were dam raised because they will already see you as the food giver and will most likely follow you around anyway. Again, it is not impossible to train a doe-raised kid but you should build a bond first by taking them away from the other goats and spending time with them on your own until they are used to you.

If you have an aggressive or not very friendly or co-operative goat then the things listed below may not work for you. Like people, all goats are different and what works for one doesn't necessarily work for another – goat training can be fun though so it's always worth a try!

Food

You may have heard the saying "a way to a man's heart is through his stomach" and the same is true for goats; these animals will do pretty much anything if food is on offer, especially if it's something they really love.

My advice is before training, find out which treats your goat particularly enjoys and use those for training. Examples include apple, second cut hay, raisins, small carrots, small pieces of garlic, small amounts of grain, banana peel, corn chips, animal crackers (for those in the USA) or other fruits and vegetables.

Patience

Your goat isn't instantly going to understand what you want them to do and you will need a lot of patience when teaching your goat anything, even if it's just getting them used to the milk stand or walking them round on a leash. Rather than spending an hour or so on one trick and expecting them to learn it, the key is to show them what you want them to do, give them a treat, repeat the behavior and then let them go off and do whatever they want to and return later in the day to repeat the training.

Your goat may be in a piggish mood and not want to work with you – if this is the case, rather than lose your temper, simply stop, take a deep breath and try again. If they are still being stubborn then leave it and try again at another time.

Training should be fun for both you and your goat. Don't hit your goat or yell at them because this will make them nervous and less likely to trust you.

Basic Training

So you have food and you have patience, so what can you teach your goat to do? Before you do any tricks you should give them basic training, which is walking on a leash and standing at a milking stand.

Leash Training

If you are planning on attending shows then leash training is crucial because you will need to lead them around a ring, so teaching them beforehand will make them easier to handle in front of a judge. Even if you don't want to attend any shows, leash training is still helpful, as it makes it easier to move your goats from one place to another if you need to and will get them used to following simple commands. Start by letting them get used to a collar – put one on and then give them a treat. If they seem happy with the collar on then add a leash and give a gentle tug.

Move slowly and don't pull too hard; you want to coax them to move but don't want to choke or strangle them. If your goat takes a few steps then give them a treat.

Repeat this for a few minutes each day, waiting until they take more and more steps each time until you give them a treat.

Milking Stand
As a pet owner, you may not be breeding or milking your goat but you may use a milking stand or something similar to trim their hooves.

Whilst goats love to climb, for some reason they are not too enamored to be put in a milking stand, so if you are going to be using one of these for whatever reason then start by walking them to the stand a few times a day just so they can see it, giving them a treat when they get there.

The best milking stands are those with a feeding bowl at the front, once they start to associate this with food they will begin to go willingly and eventually you should be able to coax them onto the stand.

Once you get them onto the stand, start getting them used to being touched by picking up their hooves if you are going to be hoof trimming. If you are planning to milk, then start getting them used to you touching their udders. If your doe is already lactating, just do short milking sessions, little and often until she is used to it.

Soon they should be happy to get onto the stand and will eat their food whilst you are doing whatever it is you need to do. If this isn't the case and you find that even after training your goat still kicks a lot, then you may consider purchasing hobbles. These are canvas straps that fasten around the goats' legs with Velcro above the knee. The hobbles hold the goats' legs together, which makes it harder for them to kick or buck although they may still be able to jump and move about.

Anglo Nubians are so smart that once you have shown them the correct way to stand on a milking stand you may find that they just take themselves off when they are ready to be milked and you will come out to find them waiting for you!

Teaching The Word "No"

Something I have found is that people think it's funny or cute when their goat runs at them and jumps. Whilst it is sweet when a baby goat jumps on your back, you don't want a bigger goat charging at you (especially if you decide to keep the horns) so I would always start to teach them 'no' when it is doing something you don't want it to do. For example, if your goat starts to be pushy and shoves at you because it wants treats or if it steals food or is climbing on the fence, etc. Whilst it is fine to train your goat with treats, it needs to learn that you give treats when they carry out certain behavior and not just because they demand it.

As well as saying "no", move the goat away from whatever it is it's doing, so if it is near the fence say "no" and move it away. If it is pushing or jumping up at you, then say no and firmly move it away. Another way to reinforce "no" is to squirt it with a water bottle.

If you are teaching "no" then correct the behavior every time it displays it. Your goat will become confused if you let it climb on the fence some days and not others.

Fun Tricks

There are plenty of different tricks you can teach your goat once they have gotten used to leash training. This can include shaking hands or 'high fives', jumping through hoops, ringing bells, walking in and out of your legs, standing or walking on their back legs, walking across a balance beam or running an agility course. Whilst I've listed a few I'm sure there are plenty others that you could find to teach your goat, but I think the principle is mainly the same for each.

These tricks can be taught in a variety of different ways; some people will use a clicker, others may use an animal training stick. My preference is with food and voice commands, but if these don't work for you and your goats then you may find an alternative way that works better.

Standing On Hind Legs Or 'Dancing'
Choose a cue word such as 'stand' or 'dance', then say this clearly and firmly whilst holding a treat above your goat's head.

You may want to first hold the treat in front of your goat's face so that they take notice of it and then slowly lift it upwards and back in a straight line. Your goat should follow it until eventually they lift their front feet off the ground.

If they don't lift their front legs, you can gently lift their front legs up for them the first few times to show your goat what you want them to do.

As soon as they are on their hind legs give them a treat. Repeat a couple of times, then let them go off and do other goat things.

Once you've done this over several days your goat should start to anticipate the treat and stand on their back legs as soon as they hear the cue word.

Once they've learnt this trick you can teach high five, sit and shaking hands in much the same way.

Jumping Through Hoops
Again, choose a cue word such as 'jump' and hold out a hula-hoop in front of your goat a little way off the ground. On the other side of the hoop hold out a treat and your goat should jump through the hoop to get it. Again. repeat daily until they can do this just by hearing the cue word.

If you want to add some pizazz to your trick, you can add streamers to your hoop once they have gotten used to jumping through it on command or you can start to cover your hoop with paper a bit at a time until there is just a small gap in the center for them to jump through – eventually you should be able to cover this up with tissue paper or thin paper with the words 'ta da' written on it. As the goat jumps through the paper will tear but it looks impressive to onlookers as they see your goat leap through a covered hoop!

Beam Walking
Goats tend to believe that the best way to get to what they want is to move in a straight line, which is why they are fairly easy to train especially with tricks such as standing on their hind legs, jumping through hoops and walking along beams.

To teach them to walk over a beam, simply lead them up to the top of the beam, then go and stand at the other end and place a treat there. Make sure they see you do this. Your goat should simply walk across the beam to get the treat.

In the beginning, if you prefer you could stand at the side of the beam a little way in front of them and hold the treat out, moving slowly so that they have to walk across the beam. Use a cue word so that eventually they will start to walk simply by hearing this word.

Ring A Bell
To teach this trick you want the goat to learn that when the bell rings it will get a treat, so to start off just ring the bell yourself a couple of times, each time it rings give your goat a small treat.

If you want the goat to ring the bell with its head, hold the bell in front of the goat at head height and hold a treat right next to it. Choose a cue word such as "ring" or "ring bell" or "make noise" then wait for the goat to touch the bell with its head. As soon as it does this, give them the treat, even if you have to move the bell with your hand in order for it to ring. The main thing you want the goat to learn at this point is that the bell rings when they touch it. Repeat this a few times until you think your goat has understood the trick. Always give the command and hold the bell close until the goat understands the trick, then if you want to you can mount the bell on a post so that you don't have to hold it. You still need to make a fuss and give a treat as soon as the goat touches the bell.

If you want the goat to ring the bell with it's foot then you will need to teach it how to shake hands first. Hold the bell in front of the goat and give the command for shake hands followed by the cue for ringing the bell so this might be "shake and ring" or something. When the goat lifts its leg up for the shake hands command move the bell in front of its hoof so that it touches it, then give lots of praise and a treat. Again you may have to move the bell with your hand at the same time to get it to ring when the goat touches it. Repeat a few times then just give the command for ringing the bell once you think the goat has understood the trick.

Once you've repeated enough times that you think the goat has understood, move the bell a bit further away rather than directly by its head or leg. Give the command and the goat should move towards the bell and ring it.

Tips

Whilst you probably want to train both your pet goats, only train one goat at a time. Have a small area where you take each goat to train them. Whilst the other may watch and learn this way, you want to make sure you are teaching them one on one, otherwise you may find the goats just play and bond with each other rather than you. You may choose to teach one goat a trick over a few days and then work with the other one or you may decide to spend a few minutes with each goat separately every day.

Keep your training sessions short. If you try and train them for hours at a time then not only will your goats get frustrated and bored but so will you. It is far better to have a few minutes repeated throughout the day.

Teach, treat, repeat – repetitiveness is the key to success, go over and over a trick several times a day and eventually your goats will understand what you want of them.

Always treat and praise your goat when it does something you want such as walking a beam, jumping through a hoop or ringing a bell, especially when it starts to do these things simply by hearing the cue words.

Don't reward bad behavior – if your goat is being pushy for a treat or jumping up at you don't give it to them. Just as you reinforce good behavior with a treat, if you treat bad behavior this will make the goat think it is doing something good.

Keep your cue words different for each trick and try not to use similar words or ambiguous words like 'okay', as we often find ourselves saying words such as 'okay' for lots of different reasons and this can confuse your goat.

Try to bond with your goats before even attempting any training. If you have bottle fed kids then you are already bonding and well on your way to being able to train them, but if you do have kids that were doe fed then rather than just going into their pen to feed and water them, hold their feed dishes and spend time in their enclosure with them to get them used to you being around.

Don't pull your goats – if you find they are not moving, for example when you are leash training, rather than pull them, try pushing gently from behind.

Conclusion

Anglo Nubian Goats make such adorable pets; they're cute, playful and can be very friendly. Although they are increasing in popularity, they are still quite unusual to find as pets, so if you are looking for an animal that is different from your ordinary dog or cat then these goats might be for you. In terms of affection and fun they can be as good as a dog or a cat whilst being a bit more exotic.

However, you need to put your animals' priority first and this means making sure you have enough space for them to roam as well as a shelter and plenty of toys to keep them occupied. If you only have a small back garden then goats may not be for you.

Unfortunately, one goat by itself will not thrive or be happy, no matter what breed it is. You can be attentive to their needs and spend hours and hours with them yet they will still be stressed and unhappy. An Anglo Nubian Goat on it's own can be very loud but not only that it can also develop health problems. You need a minimum of two goats, which means double the space, double the price and double the food costs. If one goat dies, you will need to replace it, so you should consider whether you are prepared to make such a long-term commitment.

When it comes to costs, the initial money you have to spend can be quite high – you have to buy two goats minimum, ensure you have a suitable fence, build a suitable shelter and you may even need to add a store cupboard. Add to this the cost of toys, hay rack, water troughs, brushes, milking stand, leashes and collars and so on and you could be looking at nearly a thousand pounds/dollars or more depending on the price you pay for your goats. However, the monthly costs can be fairly low and you can keep these down if you purchase hay in bulk (although this may not be realistic if you only have a small space in which to keep it). To put it into context, when I once asked an experienced breeder how much space an Anglo Nubian Goat would need they told me it is slightly less than a tennis court. This may seem small but when you think about it, actually compared to the size of some people's back gardens nowadays this is a lot!

One thing you should remember before you purchase your goats is to check the laws in your area. In the UK, some new build estates don't allow animals such as goats and chickens because they are classed as livestock. In the USA, there are also laws governing whether you can keep these or how you are to care for them. It is always better to be safe than sorry and you should make sure you are complying; the last thing you want is to buy a couple of goats, get attached and then find your neighbors have reported you to the local authorities.

The concept of keeping a goat as a pet can be quite daunting if you have never had these animals before, but as long as you do your research on what they eat and feed them the correct type of foods in the right amounts, you shouldn't have any problems. Understanding how their stomachs work is an important part of being able to keep them healthy. Remember, introduce new foods one at a time and slowly.

From a safety point of view, never tether your goats. You may feel that this keeps them safe but actually the opposite is true; tethering makes them sitting prey for predators or even other goats in the herd. It also makes them a danger to themselves as a goat most likely won't sit still for very long but rather it will get bored and try to find a way to get loose which could lead to it becoming tangled.

At night you should always lock them up, again this is to keep them safe from predators but also keeps them warm and safe, away from the rain. Goats hate to get wet and are susceptible to Pneumonia and Hypothermia so locking them in a shelter at night will ensure that they are protected from the elements as well as any other animals that may be looking for a midnight snack.

If you do purchase these goats, they can be lots of fun. You can take them to shows or just train them to do tricks at home for your own amusement if you wish to do so. They are very smart and if you repeat things over and over they will soon grasp what you want them to do. Whilst there are a few tricks listed in this book, there are also many more that you can teach them if you wish to do so.

My final thought on keeping Anglo Nubian Goats (or any goat really) is that although you will no doubt love them as a pet and maybe see them as no different to a cat or a dog, please remember that they are livestock and as such belong outside. Whilst they may come inside for a short while if you want to do so, it is far better for them to be outside with their other goat friends than inside with humans. If you want to cuddle and play with them, do so in their own enclosure.

Printed in Great Britain
by Amazon